# Model Railway Constructor

## ANNUAL 1983

*Edited by Chris Leigh*

LONDON

IAN ALLAN LTD

£3.95

# Contents

First published 1982

ISBN 0 7110 1233 4



Published by Ian Allan Ltd, Shepperton, Surrey; and printed by Ian Allan Printing Ltd at their works at Coombelands in Runnymede, England

**Front cover: 'Black Five' 4-6-0 No 5156 heads GWR stock on Ken Longbottom's 7mm scale Diggle, Halebarns and Westport layout.** *Brian Monaghan*

**Back cover, top: Oregon & Western 4-6-0 No 20, a Nickel Plate Products Class K-2 of the Burlington RR crosses the timber trestle on Leslie Tindall's HO layout.**

**Back cover, bottom: A scene at Bowland Bridge on Bernard Greaves' OO gauge LNWR layout.** *Brian Monaghan*

**Right: Flashback. Festiniog Railway 0-4-0ST *Prince* approaches Tan-y-Bwlch on a scenic module built for a magazine cover. See the article *Cover Story*.**

# Introduction

The editor of *Model Railway Constructor Annual* faces a number of problems when he starts to plan each edition. The preparation time for a book is considerably longer than for a magazine, so although *MRC Annual* should be designed to appeal to readers of the monthly *Model Railway Constructor*, it is not possible to incorporate any of the magazine's 'news' features. The annual, therefore, has to concentrate on feature articles. These need to cover a diversity of subjects to suit all tastes and scales.

In compiling this annual, I have taken a number of themes which can be traced through various different articles. It seems to me that in the absence of 'news' content, the *MRC Annual* should provide ideas for the modeller by taking a deeper look at some particular aspects, and by setting out some projects which, I hope, will encourage the reader to get out his modelling tool kit.

Ideas for layouts are covered in 'Overspill', 'Lillooet' and 'Thunders Hill'. Each is different — a railway map that might have been, a layout prototype with lots of operating potential in a far off land, and a layout scheme that works, based on a station that is almost fiction. Small scratch-building projects appeal to many modellers and simple railway structures which can be highly detailed make an attractive addition to a layout. Several suitable subjects are covered, with photographs and scale drawings, under the 'Small structures' heading. 'Datafile' includes a random selection of locomotives and items of rolling stock, and provides a simple scale diagram and photographs to fill the requirements of basic model-making research.

Locomotives and rolling stock feature in practical construction and conversion articles on the Class 47 diesel, and an engineers' train, and prototype vehicles are covered in 'Departmental coaches' and 'BR Plate Wagons'. There are also some easy electronics projects and a glimpse behind the *MRC* cover scenes of the 1960s. These days, of course, the *MRC* cover carries a full colour photograph and colour accuracy is an important feature of modelling. Any photograph of a model will tend to show up its flaws and defects, and colour adds another dimension, particularly as the reproduction of colour in photographs can be affected by lighting. The colour views used on this annual demonstrate attainable levels of realism, enhanced by colour.

These days the modeller working in the more popular scales has a wide choice of well designed and accurate models, backed up by an array of parts and accessories which is continually expanding. All this has tended to simplify the hobby to the point where some of the 'creativity' is removed. It is no longer necessary to build one's favourite locomotive if it is available ready-to-run and superbly detailed in plastic. Creating the right atmosphere of region or historical period is now just a matter of gathering together the right cast metal accessories. Thus, there is no longer such an incentive for modellers to write magazine articles describing how they built, converted or modified a particular model. Despite this bonanza of good quality models from the manufacturers, resourceful modellers are still finding ways to express their talents, and there are some remarkably fine layouts about.

With so many, perhaps even too many, magazines chasing too few articles the scope of coverage has widened to include foreign prototype material, 'non-railway' scenic items and structures, road vehicles and so on. To some, these subjects may appear irrelevant or of trivial interest, but once he moves on from a circle of track on a bare baseboard the modeller enters a world of unlimited model-making. A real railway runs through an environment which contains all these apparently unrelated subjects and therefore, a model railway should do the same. Thus, the modeller can find ideas and items of interest in an article which, at first sight, is totally unrelated to his particular sphere of interest. Perhaps, in modern parlance, today's railway modeller could say that he is 'into total modelling'.

# Cover story

Readers of *Model Railway Constructor* during the 1960s will no doubt remember the changes in style and presentation of the magazine which took place in 1964. There was a mixed reaction to the changes in graphic design which occurred at that time, but behind the scenes a less obvious change had also taken place. For the first time, *MRC* had sufficient staff to enable some major modelling projects to be undertaken in the office. The most obvious area for attention was the cover scene. Cover illustrations have always been a problem area for model magazines, since most photographs of models or layouts tend to be horizontal or 'landscape' format — wide, but not very tall. The shape of magazines, however, requires a cover illustration to be either in the vertical format, or at least square. Clearly, if *MRC* produced its own cover illustrations they could be designed to suit the cover shape, while the subject matter could, when desired, be matched to the content.

So, an *ad hoc* team, comprising editorial staff, modeller, photographer, and staff artist came together to work out ideas. The need for twelve new, different and exciting subjects each year posed a formidable challenge in itself. When the requirements of artistic design, photography and practical model-making were thrown in, the job became fascinating, enjoyable and frequently quite hilarious. Every picture tells a story, and I think that some of the stories behind those pictures can now be told without revealing any dark secrets. Some of the techniques may be of interest to modellers and photographers, even after all this time, while other stories just help to prove that modelling for pleasure or business can still be fun. For the protection of the innocent none of the leading characters is identified by name!

**Above: The Trix 'Warship' featured on the cover of the April 1965 *MRC*, with a string of hopper wagons passing on the adjacent line.**

A start was made with the September 1964 issue, but it was not until December that the first 'epic' was undertaken. The theme was to be Christmas mail trains, and since this was the

23

23

twilight era of main line steam, an appropriate Southern Region main line location was selected. To give the picture the necessary height it was decided that the model set-piece should include an over-line signalbox in the style of the one at Clapham Junction, but not actually representing any particular prototype. Thus, the basic set-up was established, but then the art and photographic representatives on the team made their contribution. In order to have a suitably wintry atmosphere, the picture should be a night scene with a cold, misty look. A small baseboard with a complex of trackwork was already available and the signalbox was installed using balsa wood and parts from an Airfix signal gantry kit. Illumination was provided by some working model lamps and signals. Numerous views were to be taken from various angles and some involved a rear three-quarter view of the Bulleid 'West Country' 4-6-2. To lend further atmosphere, the firebox door of the Kitmaster model was drilled out and a red bulb was installed in the firebox. The resulting 'firebox glow' was subsequently to be introduced on certain proprietary models!

The actual photography took place after hours, since we had to wait until dark, and the customary system of tripod-mounted camera, cable-release and long time-exposure was used. The 'mist' was cigarette smoke blown gently across the model during the exposure. Smoke and mist effects were destined to become a feature of several of the cover scenes, and various methods were tried. A polythene tube passed through the baseboard and up under the chimney of the locomotive proved particularly effective as a means of getting the smoke into the right place. Concealing the pipe between the baseboard and the underside of the locomotive chassis sometimes caused a few headaches. The smoke was provided by one cigarette smoker on the team, who would exhale his smoke down the tube. Difficulties would occur in trying to time the smoke release to coincide with the delayed action opening of the shutter on the camera. Frequently it would be necessary to shoot a whole reel of twelve negatives to be sure of getting the right effect. By the time exposure number twelve was reached, our smoker was often way past the end of his cigarette, and choking hard on the acrid fumes of a burning filter tip! In those days there were no government health warnings!

The January 1965 scene demonstrated the influence of the photographic side. The theme was simply a spin-off from an article on BR standard Class 9F 2-10-0s, and featured a suitably begrimed Kitmaster model. The smoke was provided by a photograph of a locomotive (an LMS '8F'!) working hard, carefully posed behind the model. Careful selection of the photograph was most important since very few of the cover photographs were retouched in any way. Techniques of lighting and camera angle were used to advantage but any 'cheating' on the final result was frowned upon. What you saw, was what you got.

Most editors like to feature a snow scene on their magazine cover at least once during the winter, and the editor of *MRC* was no exception. Model makers, on the other hand, tend to resent creating a detailed model only to have most of the detail obliterated by white powder! The February

**Left and below left: Alternatives for the night parcels train scene featured on the December 1964 cover.**

**Below: Only the lamp-post and the smoke were 'real' in this view of a grimy Kitmaster '9F' 2-10-0 apparently working hard.**

cover combined snow with an experiment in light and shade. A Wills '4F' fitted with a Plastikard snowplough was posed amid some sidings. The only accessories were a buffer stop, water tank and a few people. For many years salt had been recommended for model snow, but our experience soon showed that it would not cling to sloping surfaces in the way that snow does. A solution was found in Ajax, the cleaning powder, which at that time was free of any 'coloured' additives. A sprinkling of Ajax, and a single carefully positioned light source to provide the shadows, completed the scene. The bird's eye viewpoint was achieved by placing the model on the floor, which made the placing of the light source rather difficult. Worse still, the photographer had to be a contortionist to look through the viewfinder, while the strong smell of Ajax lingered in the office for ages, and must have puzzled many visitors!

A combination of model work posed against a photograph of the prototype was used for the next month and was not particularly memorable. Not so the April cover, where the theme was to be an article on the Trix 'Warship' diesel. A broadside of a speeding subject is known among photographers as a 'panned' shot and our first attempts to photograph the Trix model at speed were a total disaster. The main problem was that even on the best laid track the model would have a certain amount of vertical bounce which was not apparent to the naked eye, but which produced a blurred photograph. In the panned shot, the scenery, and not the model, had to be blurred. So, for the first time, we were beaten and went back to the drawing board. Our photographer

**Left: The infamous water-trough scene from October 1965.**

**Above: A 'panned' shot of a Hornby-Dublo 'Castle' 4-6-0 which was actually running under power.**

then produced the answer, and created a model-making problem for which he was not well-loved! The scenery must be made to move, while the locomotive stayed still. This would have been fairly straightforward but for the fact that even the track on which the model stood was required to move.

Eventually the rear half of the locomotive was attached to some woodwork situated 'off camera', while the baseboard and scenery was made to roll as a unit over several sections of sawn-off broom handle. The gear-drive of the model was removed so that the wheels would turn, and only a couple of inches movement of the scenery during the time-exposure, was needed to create the effect of speed. How it would have benefited from one of the recent super-detailed 'Warship' models!

The next modelling challenge came with the June issue when the theme was inspection pits and the then new Wills 'N7' 0-6-2T was the main subject. The idea was simple — a view of the locomotive taken by a photographer apparently standing in the inspection pit. However, full-size cameras will not fit 4mm scale inspection pits so the effect was achieved by widening the inspection pit gradually throughout its length until the lens would fit between its walls. The focal length of the camera was such that the pit had to be over two feet long if the locomotive was to be in focus. The rest was simple because the shed door was a cut-out in a sheet of black card, three suitable figures were modified for their tasks, and the finished print was retouched to disguise the gear-wheel.

Straightforward modelling projects featured for the next months but then an article on water troughs provided the impetus for an October cover scene which caused some real fun. The new Bec 'Director' 4-4-0 was to be featured picking up water from the model troughs and to give the impression of movement the 'moving scenery and stationary train' dodge was to be tried again. A new twist was given to the success which we had been having with steam and smoke effects created by blowing cigarette smoke through a polythene tube. This time the effect of water spraying from the tender was to be created by blowing water through the strategically placed tube.

Exactly who was to blame for this brain-wave is now forgotten, but the culprit should have known that real water cannot be scaled down to model proportions. With the scene set up and gently moving in front of the camera, the polythene tube was carefully filled with water and one member of the team then filled his lungs and gave an enormous blow down the pipe. The

**Left: Final choice for the inspection pit scene.**

**Below: The Trix 'Western' posed in a night scene in which the 'wet' platform is particularly effective.**

**Right: One of the rejected prints of the Wills 'N7' over the inspection pit. The 'water' in the pit has worked well but there is an unnatural gap in the pit-wall on the right.**

**Below right: Winter in the north-east and a Wills '4F' has become stuck in a substantial snowdrift of Ajax.**

heavy cast metal tender sailed through the air and the scenery and onlookers in the room were drenched in half a pint of cold water! To add insult to injury, the early fibre-based flexible track used on the model soaked up the water like a sponge and distorted out of all recognition. The final version of the cover, posed on rebuilt scenery, returned to the more satisfactory use of the polythene tube for a smoke effect.

In the wintry scene featured on the December 1965 cover a Trix 'Western' diesel was posed against a painted background representing the roof of, perhaps, Paddington or Bristol. The smoke tube was connected to the locomotive exhaust port to give a smoke effect suitable to a departing 'Western' and extensive use was made of glycerine to simulate a really wet evening. It worked well.

The year 1966 saw the introduction of a frontispiece as a regular feature, and this brought the need for a second photograph, while the introduction of curious coloured papers posed further problems. January featured overhead electrification, with another panned shot, but this time without the moving scenery method.

The motive power depot featured in March was one of the most extensive modelling jobs, but in some ways it simply proved that the best ideas were the simplest ones. The sequence of silhouettes in May, for instance, was much more striking.

By the middle of the year it was proving difficult to sustain the supply of new ideas and new techniques and November saw the first reversion to use of a model not produced in the office. It broke new ground in not featuring a train in a prominent position, and for a while we wondered what the reaction might be. We need not have worried. Attention then turned to more substantial modelling projects such as a harbour, terminus and airport as it became increasingly difficult to justify the expense of so much time and effort just for a cover illustration. During 1967 some of these projects provided cover scenes as well as material for feature articles, while a change of editorial approach saw a return to conventional photography on the magazine cover.

In the two years, those covers received a mixed reaction. Some loved them, a few hated them, but they were very much a product of the time and reflected the then-new cult of fashionable graphic design. From a modelling viewpoint I like to think that they helped to push back the frontiers of the hobby a little, and even today they represent one of very few attempts to use model railway subjects to achieve special photographic effects.

Datafile 1

# Midland & South Western Junction Railway 2-6-0

The two 'Moguls' supplied by Beyer-Peacock to the MSWJR must surely have been the prettiest locomotives of their type ever to have worked in England. No 16 earned the rather uncomplimentary nickname 'Galloping Alice' doubtless due to the appearance created by the small wheels when running at speed. The following information from *The Locomotive Magazine* of 1902 gives the information in a pleasantly appropriate style.

'A more powerful engine being required for the heavy goods trains that run from Southampton to the north via Cheltenham, No 14 was obtained from Messrs Beyer, Peacock & Co who had on hand an engine suitable for the company's requirements. This had been built for a railway in the South American continent. It is of the Mogul

**Below: MSWJR 2-6-0 No 16 in original condition. Note the placing of the front frames and buffer beam. Curiously, the original tracing from which these drawings were made, shows 'Ross'-type safety valves.**
*LPC/Ian Allan Library*

**Above: No 16 in unlined black livery with MSWJR lettering in script style.** *L&GRP No 14110*

**Left: The right-hand side of No 14 showing the smaller cab, and the crosshead-driven pump. No photographs showing this side of No 16 have come to light, but it must be assumed that the same arrangement was employed.** *Bucknall Collection/Ian Allan Library*

type, having six wheels coupled, a leading pony truck and outside cylinders. Until the Midland and Great Northern Companies obtained their Moguls from America this was the sole example in England, if we except those built for the Great Eastern Railway from the designs of Mr Adams, but all now broken up. This engine was No 3679 on the makers' list, and has cylinders 18in diameter placed horizontally with a 26in stroke. The piston rods are tailed through the front covers. The pony truck has 2ft 9in diameter wheels, the coupled wheels being 4ft diameter; the total wheelbase is 19ft, the fixed wheelbase being only 11ft. The pony truck centre to the leading wheel centre is 8ft, leading to driving centres 5ft 7in and driving to trailing centres 5ft 5in. The firebox being rather long, the trailing axle passes beneath it. The outside diameter of the boiler is 4ft 5in, the length of the barrel 10ft 4in, and the centre line is 6ft 9in above the rail level. The length of the firebox casing is 6ft 7in. The boiler is fed by one injector and one pump worked from the piston crosshead outside the right hand set of wheels. The tubes afford 1,050sq ft of heating surface, the firebox 93sq ft the total heating surface being 1,143sq ft. The firegrate area is 20.8sq ft. The total weight in working order is 43 tons 2cwt 1qr distributed thus: On pony truck 6 tons 14cwt, on the leading wheels 12 tons 2qrs, on the driving wheels 12 tons 6cwt. 3qrs, and on the trailing wheels 12 tons 1cwt. This engine is also fitted with steam brake and Ramsbottom's safety valves. The cab is rather small and the roof overhanging the weather board too much spoils the appearance. The number of the engine is in brass figures riveted to the cab sides. The valve motion is reversed by a wheel and screw placed on the right hand side of the engine. This engine proved so satisfactory that another similar was ordered by the company from the same builders in 1896. It is numbered 16, the makers' number being 3884; it is identical with No 14, excepting that the cab is larger, and that the trailing end overhangs further. The tenders for these engines have six wheels 3ft 6½in diameter, the wheelbase being 11ft; from the trailing engine wheel to the leading tender wheel is 9ft 2in. The total wheelbase of the engine and tender is 39ft 2in. The tender carries 2,000 gallons of water and 3 tons of fuel; its weight loaded is 22 tons 11cwt, the total weight of engine and tender in working order being thus 65 tons 13cwt 1qr. No 14 is stationed at Cheltenham and No 16 at Andover Junction.'

The latter passed into GWR ownership in 1923 and was rebuilt with a Swindon domed boiler and a standard GWR tender. In that form it lasted until withdrawal in 1930. No 14 was withdrawn by the MSWJR in 1914 and sold minus its boiler four years later. It was provided with a new cab and boiler and worked until 1943 at Cramlington and Hartley Main collieries in the north-east.

The simple outline diagram included here is taken from a tracing of an official drawing marked 'Cirencester Locomotive Works, December 13th, 1902' which was in my possession for a short while. It depicts No 16, but the cab of No 14 is also shown. The short cab reduced the length of this locomotive to 47ft 3in over buffers. Livery was olive green, lined in yellow and black with the MSWJR lettering in either block capitals or script. During wartime, an unlined black livery was used.

**Below: No 16 in GWR condition with new boiler and tender.** *LPC/Ian Allan Library*

*Drawing 4mm:1ft scale*

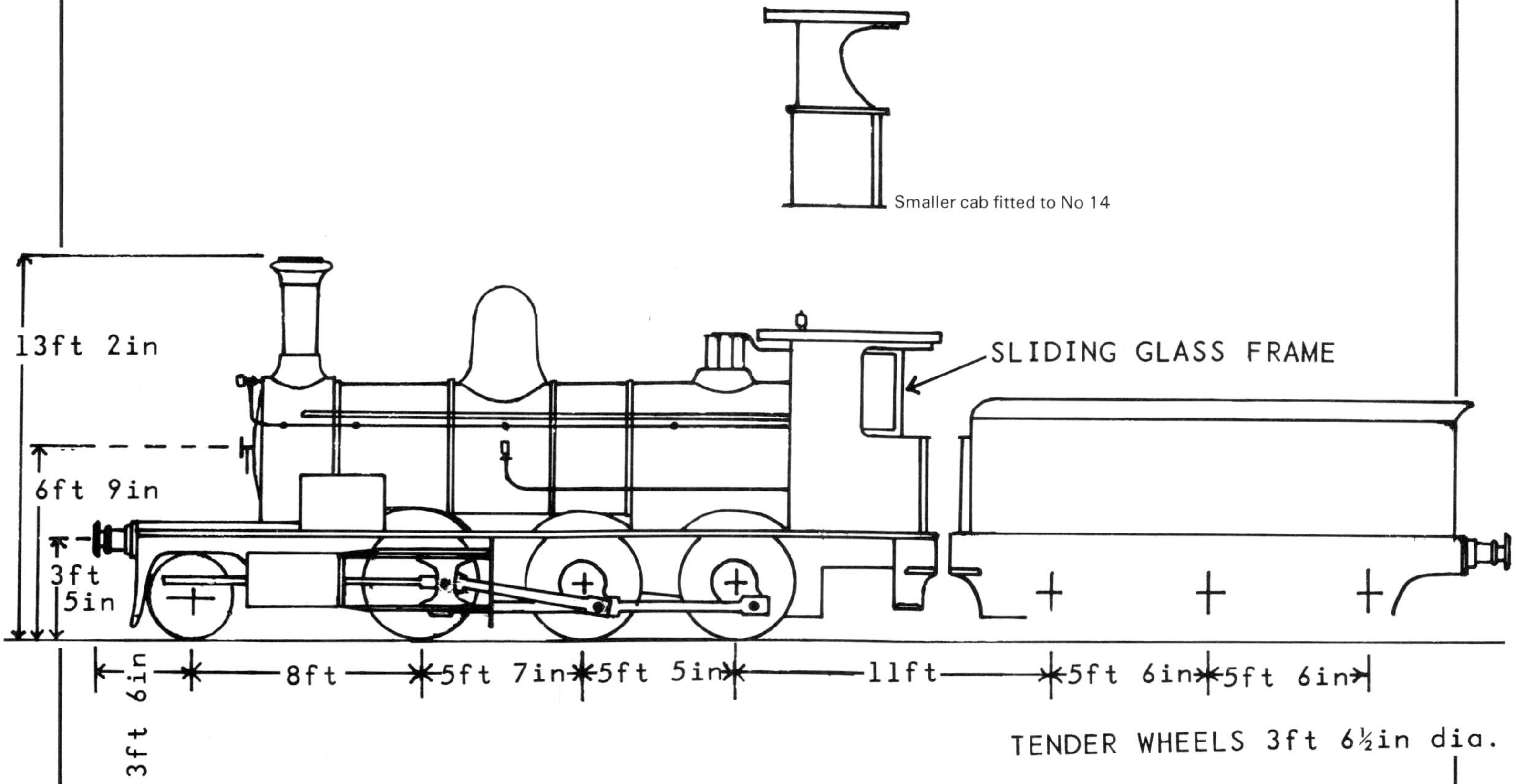

# A personal souvenir

## *Charles Phillips* modifies the Hornby Class 47

Few people can fail to have been moved by all the pomp and pageantry of the Royal wedding on 29 July 1981. In particular, the departure of the Prince and Princess of Wales by train to commence their honeymoon brought great pleasure and pride to thousands of railwaymen and railway enthusiasts. It was natural that these people would be keen to have a rail-oriented souvenir of the happy day and several manufacturers introduced suitable models painted in appropriate 'wedding' colour schemes. One favourite of the manufacturers was the Brush Class 47 diesel locomotive which had been named *Lady Diana Spencer* a few weeks before the wedding.

I guess I should have known that Hornby would do it, but as I walked back from watching the Royal special train pass through Weybridge I was blissfully unaware that such a model was contemplated. Having satisfied myself that I wanted to build a wedding souvenir, and having decided that the electro-diesel and special saloon was really too complex a scratch-building job, I settled upon the idea of modifying and repainting a Hornby Class 47. I had always been puzzled that little had been written in the model press about Hornby's model of the ubiquitous 47. After all, every modern image layout needs at least one, and the Hornby model looked reasonably accurate.

I purchased one of the green examples named *Mammoth* (then the only colour scheme produced by Hornby) and set about the task of converting it into No 47.712 *Lady Diana Spencer*. The work involved some fairly substantial detail modification and a complete repaint. However, the only extras required for the job, were a set of screw couplings, an SMS transfer sheet, and a pair of the excellent etched nameplates from LFC Models of Holmfirth, Huddersfield.

No 47.712 was the last of a batch of twelve Class 47/4 locomotives (the variant with electric train heating equipment) to be converted to push-pull operation for use on Glasgow-Edinburgh services. It was originally allocated the name *Prince Charles Edward* but this was never carried and eventually a competition was held in Scottish newspapers and radio to select names for Nos 47 711/2. The competition winners unveiled the nameplate of 'their' locomotives, *Greyfriars Bobby*, and *Lady Diana Spencer*, respectively. In readiness for the naming both locomotives had been repainted in the new BR standard livery of yellow cabs, grey roof and black window frames, with large logo and lettering. They looked most distinctive.

The Class 47/7s differ from other 47s in having jumper cables and pipework on the ends for push-pull operation, and a sealed beam headlight above the coupler. Within the class there are all the usual variations in the treatment of the former four-character headcode panel, although No 47.712 has this plated over, painted yellow and fitted with marker lights.

These modifications point the way to some of the work needed on the Hornby model, but it does not stop there. The model was first produced several years ago, and standards of accuracy have improved since the original moulds were made. Accordingly the model has a number of fine raised lines and mould marks which marr its appearance. In particular there are two painting

**Two views of the modified and repainted Hornby Class 47.**

guide lines along the bodysides, and various others on the ends. All these need to be removed, thus ensuring that a complete repaint will be needed, whatever the colour scheme of the original model. The bogie sideframes are a little crude, with several filled in areas which need to be filed out, and the model rides too high on its bogies. All these points can be rectified, and a much better looking 47 is the result.

I began by dismantling the locomotive, separating the body and chassis, removing the cab interiors and all the glazing pieces. Some of these are glued in place and need to be treated with care. Removal of the extraneous detail was then commenced using a sharp craft knife. Avoid the pointed knife blades as these tend to dig in to the plastic. I found that the more 'detail' I took off the ends, the more like a Class 47 it looked, so I removed all the moulded handrails and the black moulding from the headcode panel. The painting guide lines and the mould parting lines on the corners and roof dome were taken off with craft knife and fine file. I finished off by smoothing the affected areas with some 1000 grade abrasive paper.

The headcode panel was replaced with styrene sheet, drilled for the marker lights, and fixed in place with Plastruct solvent adhesive. All the end handrails and those on the cab doors were replaced with new ones made up from soft wire obtained from a craft shop. The body was drilled with a No 68 drill held in a pin chuck, and the handrails were glued into the holes with Evo-stik. The jumper cables were added from thread and small pieces of styrene sheet, and the headlights were salvaged from my scrap box. These could easily be turned up in the chuck of an electric drill. This completed work on the body.

The bodyshell was masked with adhesive tape and given three coats of Precision Paints rail blue, lightly applied with an air brush. The rest of the painting was done with a soft brush, using Humbrol matt yellow and matt black. The roof shade was a mix of matt black and white to provide a pale grey which was then 'warmed' with a dash of brown and matched to a colour photograph. The logo and lettering proved a problem, but since then the large numbers and logos have appeared in the SMS transfers range of waterslide decals. I drew my logos on the bodysides, masked them will Sellotape and applied white paint. The numbers are borrowed from a Canadian National transfer sheet. The SMS sheet makes life a lot simpler!

When the glazing material was replaced in the cabs, I found that the new colour scheme seemed to emphasise the thickness of the window pillars and the deeply recessed glazing. This impression was confirmed by local club members to whom I showed the partly completed masterpiece! I scored round each of the cab windows with a fine pointed scriber to mark the outline of the windows on the plastic glazing. I then removed the glazing, cut out the individual windows, and filed back to the scribed line. The individual pieces were then installed flush, from the outside of the window apertures and fixed with solvent adhesive. Some days later, a crazing effect appeared on the glazing where I had been careless

**Above: No 47.712 after 'shopping' at Crewe, in the new BR livery but un-named.**
*B. J. Nicolle*

**Left: The opposite end of No 47.712 *Lady Diana Spencer*, clearly showing the extra end details and the revised treatment of the former headcode panel.**
*J. E. Augustson*

**Right: Top detail of the locomotive with the first stages of grime appearing.** *C. P. Boocock*

in applying the adhesive. The effect of the flush glazing is, however, a marked improvement in the appearance.

Turning to the chassis, the main jobs here were to improve the appearance of the bogies, and to reduce the overall height of the model by some 2mm. The bogie sideframes were tackled first by unclipping them from the chassis and carving away unwanted areas. A sharp knife is the best tool for this, as the resilient plastic tends to resist filing. I removed all the brake shoes, since these are out of line with the wheel treads and I then set about carving away the main 'blind' areas where there should be daylight visible. I also took out the imitation wheel segment moulded into the inner end of each bogie, thus revealing the actual wheels. The two distinctive oval holes in the top member of each bogie were drilled out with a $^1/_{16}$in drill.

One important omission from the Hornby model is the elongated triangle of framing which is visible extending from below the cab doors to the buffer beam fairing. This is actually the only visible part of the main structural framing on the prototype. Some small pieces of styrene sheet serve the purpose on the model

Lowering the overall height of the model involves some fairly ruthless cutting, and care must be taken to ensure that it continues to sit square on the bogies. Even so, the body of the locomotive does become a rather loose fit on the bogies. These have no centre pivot and are held in place by a number of locators and clips. Part of this arrangement is visually obtrusive in the form of a curved black moulding above the centre of each bogie sideframe. This does not exist on the prototype, so I began by cutting them off the model. I then cut down each of the restraining clips on the motor bogie until it was possible to push the bogie up further into the body and eliminate the over scale gap between the two. The chassis was packed up with strips of styrene sheet in front of, and behind, the bogie to prevent excessive movement. The trailing bogie was dealt with in the same way, but in addition there is a pyramid shaped centre dimple on the underframe which must be reduced in height to allow the bogie to be repositioned. All this is much easier to do than to describe and it becomes clearer once the job is started.

The end result looks quite impressive and brings the Class 47 up to a standard which compares well with the more recent ready-to-run diesel models.

# Steam in the street

## A modeller's view of roadside tramways

Long before Rev Awdry created his immortal character *Toby* the tram engine, tramways were popular with modellers. Not the creaking wooden-bodied electric tramcars (though these certainly have a following) but the rural roadside tramway with its skirted, and often absurdly disguised, steam locomotive.

Tramways were never commonplace in the UK. They were cheap to build, using a combination of street track and light railway 'reserved' right of way, and they brought the railways right into town, close to people and into a position where frequent stops could be made.

**Below: The Bideford, Westward Ho and Appledore Railway which opened in 1902 was one of England's more absurd minor railways. It was a standard gauge system, but owing to its location, was totally divorced from neighbouring lines. Its tracks ran through the streets of Bideford to the Quay, but most of its route was away from the road on its own right of way. This is the Hunslet 2-4-2T *Kingsley*, seen at Bideford. One motion cover plate has been removed, but for modelling purposes almost any suitably sized mechanism or motor bogie could be concealed behind those side skirts. The body would make an unusual and not too difficult first project for scratch-building. Incidentally, the BWAR was the only English standard gauge line to use the centre-buffer-coupling.**
*Bucknell Collection/Ian Allan Library*

**Left: A typical BWAR train. The curious American-style coaches were built by Bristol Carriage & Wagon Co and finished in natural varnished wood. There were several vehicles, of two lengths, 46ft and 66ft. This appears to be one of the shorter vehicles. The standard of finish and fitting out was reputedly very high, but after the line closed in 1917 at least one vehicle ended its days as several beach huts! Freelance modellers might find a suitable American coach model to adapt with a more British roof. Scratch-builders may face problems since details of the BWAR and its equipment are scarce.**
*L&GRP/David & Charles*

**Centre left: The best-loved British tramway was undoubtedly the Great Eastern Railway's Wisbech & Upwell line. Here, a classic passenger tram headed by an 0-4-0T locomotive is seen in Elm Road, Wisbech. At this time the road was unsurfaced and traffic was evidently light, however stringent operating rules were laid down. The locomotives had to have a cab at each end, all moving parts, and the fire must be hidden from view, and the locomotive must consume its own steam and smoke. Hence the development of these delightful little 0-4-0T and 0-6-0T tram engines.**
*Bucknell Collection/Ian Allan Library*

**Below: Passengers boarding a tram at Upwell station, where the railway had reserved track, away from the road. The locomotive is running backwards and the pipe visible on the roof returned steam from the safety valves into the tanks so that there was no risk of a sudden blow-off frightening horses in the street. The locomotives were governed to a maximum 8mph and the safety chains on the buffer beam lasted into BR days on some locomotives.** *Bucknell Collection/Ian Allan Library*

They paid the price of suffering severe restrictions on speed and operating practices, with the result that, in these islands, passenger services on such lines were extinct by the 1930s and the last tramway of all closed in 1966.

In recent years they seem to have faded from the modelling scene too, and this is a great pity since they offer such interesting modelling opportunities. They also make some aspects of model model making very easy. If any of the prototype systems were to be closely followed, a fair amount of scratch-building would be required, but this need not be difficult. The complex working parts of the locomotives were often totally concealed behind skirting panels, and much of the trackwork was also hidden in the road surface.

This picture feature looks at some of the English tramways and suggests some appropriate model-making ideas.

**Top: At Wisbech station the trams made connection with the main line, and this is surely a perfect setting for a model railway, providing a branch connection with a difference. Note how the trackbed of the tramway is raised so that the platform is only some 14in above rail level. The tram locomotives worked over the main line to Stratford for repairs.** *Bucknell Collection/Ian Allan Library*

**Above right: The next four views of the line show specific aspects of the roadside tramway which call for special model-making care and an eye for detail. The Upwell line served a major fruit growing area and this was its main reason for survival after passenger services were withdrawn. This 1950 view shows a heavy train of fruit vans alongside the canal at Outwell. Note how the railway occupies the roadside verge on the canal bank, and also the rather overgrown state of the track. The train appears to exceed the normal permitted loadings.** *H. C. Casserley*

**Right: Swinging away from the canal, the tramway crosses the road to reach a section of reserved track. The crossing is unmarked save for a warning sign on which the familiar red triangle has been broken. The locomotive is one of the specially 'skirted' diesel shunters which took over from steam on the Upwell line.** *D. Thompson*

**Above: This road junction near Outwell Basin leads immediately across the railway and the canal. Warning signs are provided on both sides of the road, and note the white stop line placed close to the rails.** *D. Thompson*

**Below: The tramway in a townscape makes for a dramatic picture. The GER and LNER tramway locomotives were also used as dock shunters, and this one is seen in Yarmouth in 1951. Here the track is check-railed and infilled with wooden blocks. The locomotive has lost its fenders and valances, and the traditional flat-backed coal lorry is almost as much a thing of the past as the roadside tramway.** *H. C. Casserley*

# Small Structures 1

## GER Elm Bridge Tram Stop

**Right: Close-up of Class J70 0-6-0T tram locomotive No 68225 in BR black livery and still carrying safety chains. Note the weather curtains on the doors. There were few visible differences between the 0-6-0Ts and their 0-4-0T forebears, the most obvious being the curved lower edge to the valances on the J70. A white metal OO scale kit for the J70 is available.** *E. Blakey*

**Left: A marvellous modellers' view of a J70 with side valances removed. Note the open end doors, pile of coal, sliding windows, and a pair of boots hung from the lamp iron! The scene is Ipswich docks in 1946.**
*C. C. B. Herbert*

**Drawings 4mm: 1ft scale**

**Above: A freight train worked by 0-4-0T No 129 in Great Eastern days. Note the cattle wagons which have been sheeted over. The white staining is caused by the liquid used to wash the vehicle interiors.** *Real Photos*

**Centre right: A typical passenger train of the 2½ mile Wantage Tramway which linked the Berkshire village to the Great Western main line at Wantage Road station. The Matthews locomotive is thought to be unique and was probably built by Fox-Walker. A narrow gauge tram locomotive of similar appearance was once produced in H09 scale by Eggerbahn. The second passenger vehicle is a former bogie double-deck car.** *Real Photos*

**Right: Wantage Tramway No 4 was a Hughes (later Brush) 0-4-0T which latterly operated without its coupling rods, as shown here. It was scrapped about 1920, but a more conventional 0-4-0T used by the company, No 5 *Shannon*, survived the closure of the line and is now preserved at Didcot. The WT locomotives were maintained by the GWR at Swindon.** *Real Photos*

Above: With just one coal wagon and a brake van in tow, one of the diesel shunters squeals round the curve at Elm Bridge on the Wisbech & Upwell line. The buildings forming the Elm Bridge depot consisted of a small brick goods office and an open fronted wooden shelter. Drawings based upon these two structures accompany this article. *D. Thompson*

Right: The LNER 'J70' is the prototype of a delightful little locomotive kit produced by K's. It is one of their earliest models, but was reintroduced in updated form during 1981. The body is basically a box structure made up of white metal castings, and with the skirt and cow-catchers integral with the sides and ends. The mechanism is completely hidden, so the manufacturers have used some licence here, and simplified it to an inside cylinder 0-4-0. This does not cause any problems unless you wish to model the 'skirt-less' version, in which case a chassis would have to be a scratch-built to suit.

The model lends itself to some extra detailing, and in view of the fact that the new K's motor/gearbox takes up very little space inside, a boiler and firebox could be installed if desired. I began by recutting all the planking detail on the body using a steel rule and scriber, since the detail on the castings is so faint that it would tend to disappear when painted. The body was assembled following the instructions, but I then filled in the various gaps in the floor with styrene sheet. This is particularly important inside the doorways. In order to keep the cab cool in hot weather these locomotives often ran with the small end doors open, so I decided to reproduce this on one end of the model. The cast doors were drilled out and filed out to shape and new doors, from styrene sheet, were fitted in the open position. After painting, some crushed coal was added on the floor immediately inside the doors. The fireman's shovel and bucket supplied in the kit were added at this end, the latter fitted with a new wire handle and hung over the centre lamp iron. The model was glazed and fitted with screw couplings.

The former Airfix Drewry shunter kit provides an ideal basis for conversion to one of the diesel tram shunters. My example is motorised with a neat little split-frame chassis which used to be produced by Eames of Reading. However, the skirting could well be used to hide a suitable 0-4-0 or 0-6-0 chassis. Apart from the addition of skirting and cow-catchers, the main modifications to the Airfix kit involve the shape of the cab-windows and the exhaust stack.

# Wheels round the curves

*T. Crabtree*

As any railway modeller will know, a bogie or chassis carrying one or two axles is able to travel safely round any reasonable curve. Problems begin when the bogie or chassis carries three or more axles. Years ago, some manufacturers of ready to run equipment decided on an easy solution. They simply fitted flangeless wheels to all axles except the endmost. Unfortunately, this cannot be seriously considered by anyone who is seeking a true prototypical appearance.

The modern practice amongst modellers is to use flanged wheels on all axles. To allow curves to be negotiated, all axles except the endmost are allowed to float sideways. This improves the appearance of the model, but can lead to problems with connecting rods and current pickup on locomotives. The greater the sideways float allowed, the greater these problems become. The object of this article is to show a method of determining the amount of sideways float required. By limiting the float to just above that which is actually required, the problems can be minimised.

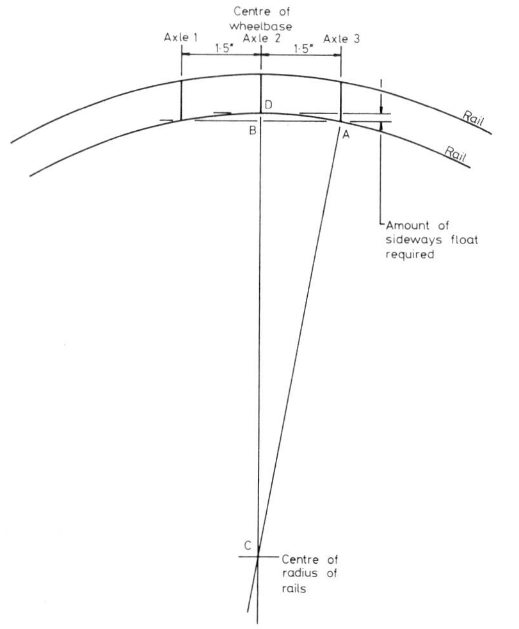


Fig.1. A CHASSIS WITH THREE EQUALLY SPACED AXLES, ON A CURVED TRACK

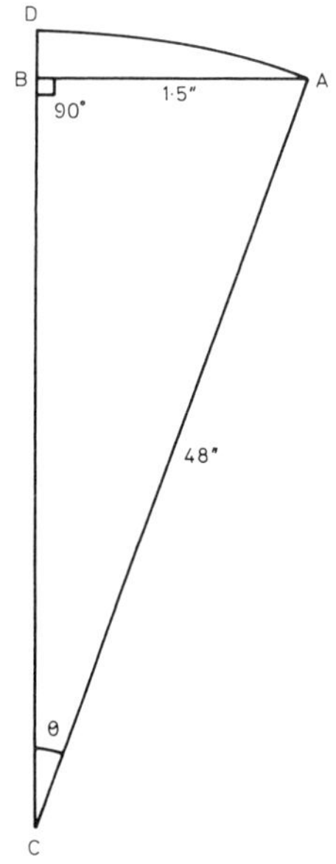


Fig.2. SIMPLIFIED DIAGRAM FOR CALCULATION (NOT TO SCALE)

## The calculation

The method of calculating the sideways float is shown in this section. A knowledge of elementary trigonometry is required, together with an electronic scientific calculator. Those not wishing to follow the calculation can move on to the next section.

Fig 1 represents a chassis with three axles on a curved track. Let us assume that the axles are spaced 1.5in apart, and that the radius of the inside rail is 48in. The diagram can be drawn more simply, as shown in Fig 2.

$$\text{Then, in triangle ABC, } \frac{AB}{AC} = \sin\theta$$

$$\therefore \frac{1.5}{48} = \sin\theta$$

$$\therefore \sin\theta = 0.03125$$

$$\therefore \theta = 1.7907847 \text{ degrees}$$

$$\text{In triangle ABC, } \frac{AB}{BC} = \tan\theta$$

$$\therefore \frac{1.5}{BC} = \tan 1.7907847$$

$$\therefore BC = \frac{1.5}{\tan 1.7907847}$$

$$= \frac{1.5}{0.0312652}$$

$$= 47.976555 \text{ inches}$$

$$\text{And } BD = CD - BC$$

$$= 48 - 47.976555$$

$$= 0.0234448 \text{ inches}$$

This is the amount of sideways float required to allow the chassis to negotiate the curve shown in Fig 1. This must now be doubled, so that the curve can be safely rounded with the chassis facing in either direction.

So total sideways float required on axle 2 is:

$$2 \times 0.0234448$$

$$= 0.0468896$$

$$= 0.047 \text{ inches}$$

In order to minimise errors, it is advisable to carry out the calculation in a single sequence. Calculators differ, but for mine (a Casio fx-31), the sequence is:

1.5 [÷] 48 [=] [INV] [sin] [tan] [1/x] [×] 1.5 [+/−] [+] 48 [=] [×] 2 [=]

Note that, in the calculation, the radius of the inside rail is used. As the radius increases, the required amount of sideways float decreases. This means that the worst condition is catered for and the calculation can be used for any gauge of model.

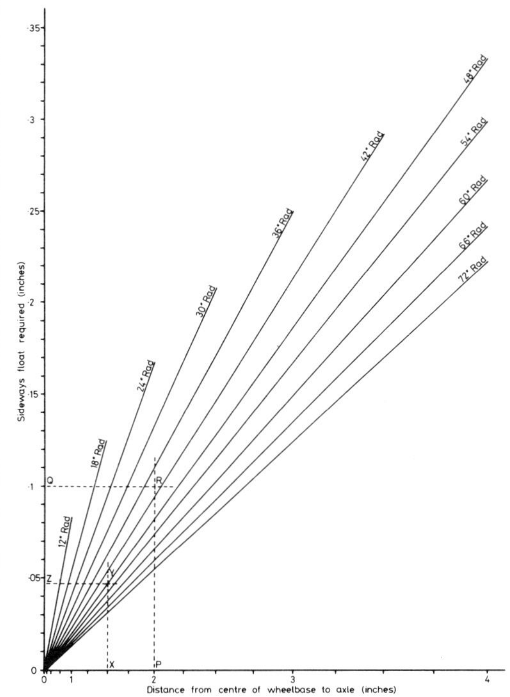


Fig.3. GRAPH RELATING SIDEWAYS FLOAT, AXLE SPACING AND TRACK RADIUS

## The Graph

The graph shown in Fig 3 was drawn after carrying out a series of calculations. In most cases, it allows the required sideways float to be found without carrying out any maths at all. For the example shown previously, the graph is used as follows:

1) The distance from the centre of the wheelbase to axle 1 or 3 is 1.5in. A mark is made on the horizontal scale at this position. This is point X. Note that this scale is divided into quarter inch steps, and that the divisions do not appear equal.
2) A vertical line is drawn through X as shown. This radius of the inside rail around which the chassis is to run is 48in. At the point where the vertical line crosses the 48in radius line, Y is marked.

3) A line is drawn through Y, to cross the vertical scale at point Z. This scale is divided equally into 0.01in steps.
4) Point Z indicates the amount of sideways float required on axle 2. In this case it is 0.047in.

**Chassis with four axles**

Because there is now no axle at the centre of the wheelbase, a slightly different method is used. Suppose that the chassis is as shown in Fig 4, and that it is to run round a curve of 48in inside radius:

For spacing of 2.25in, float is 0.106in (from graph)
For spacing of 0.75in, float is 0.012in (from graph)
Therefore, float required on axles 2 and 3 is 0.106 − 0.012
= 0.094in

A similar method can be used for a chassis with an odd number of axles which are not equally spaced. The result of this is that there is no axle at the centre of the wheelbase.

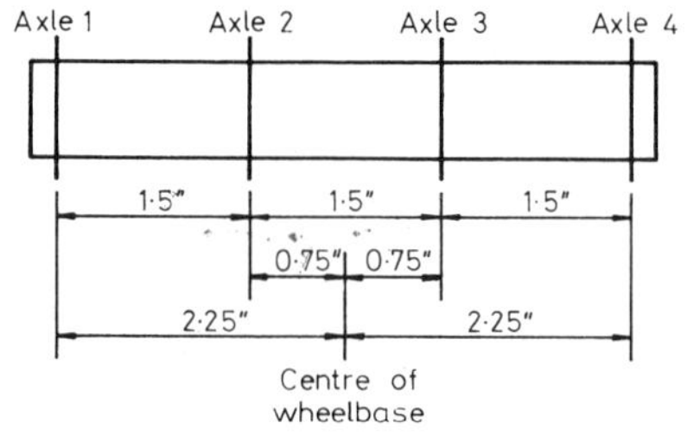


Fig.4. A CHASSIS WITH FOUR EQUALLY SPACED AXLES

**Chassis with five axles**

This type of chassis is shown in Fig 5. It may be an advantage to limit the float on axles 2 and 4 to a closer amount than on axle 3. Suppose, again, that the chassis is to run round a curve of 48in inside radius.

For spacing of 3in, float is 0.188in (from graph)
Therefore, float required on axle 3 is 0.188in
For spacing of 1.5in, float is 0.047in (from graph)
Therefore, float required on axles 2 and 4 is 0.188 − 0.047
= 0.141in

**Finding the minimum radius**

Suppose that we have a ready-built chassis. It is sometimes necessary to find the minimum radius curve around which this can safely travel. The graph can also be used for this purpose.

Let us assume that the chassis has three equally spaced axles which are each 2in apart. The sideways float on the centre axle is measured with feeler gauges, and found to be 0.100in. Using the graph, the procedure is as follows:

1) A mark is made on the horizontal scale at the 2in position. This is point P.
2) A vertical line is drawn through P as shown.
3) A mark is made on the vertical scale at the 0.100in position. This is point Q.
4) A horizontal line is drawn through Q as shown. The two lines cross at R.
5) Point R indicates the minimum radius curve around which the chassis will travel. This lies between the 36in and 42in lines. Allowing a margin for safety, 42in would be the minimum radius of the inside rail.

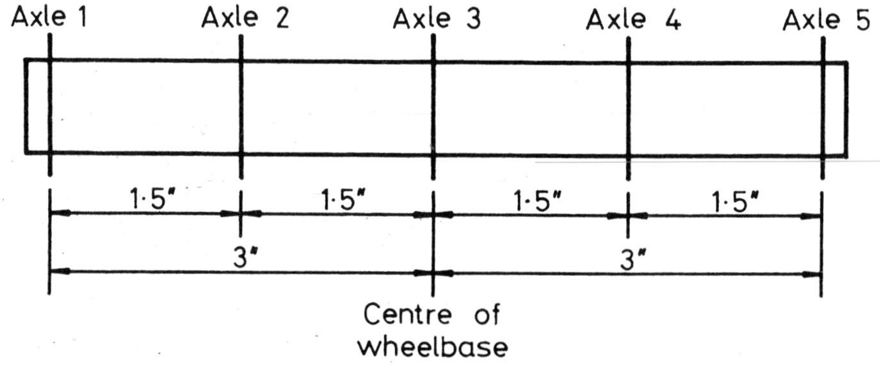


Fig.5. A CHASSIS WITH FIVE EQUALLY SPACED AXLES

# Ones that got away

This feature is not a product review by magazine standards, but rather a look at some of the products, recent and not so recent, which have slipped almost unnoticed past the reviewers in the British model magazines. The coverage of regular features such as *MRC's* Constructor's Review' is fairly thorough where British models are concerned, so most of the items covered here are of foreign manufacture.

**Mougel: SNCF couchette coach**

French manufacturer Mougel produces a number of plastic kits of French rolling stock in HO scale, including a comprehensive range of the latest Corail coaches. The range includes both the Vu B10 C10 2nd class and Vu A9 C9 1st class couchette vehicles in the form of high quality plastic kits. The body shell is a finely detailed plastic moulding which is prepainted in the correct blue and grey colour scheme. Indeed, with use of self-coloured plastic for some of the smaller parts, there is virtually no need to paint any part of this model. A printed brown card template is provided for the interior layout and this is simply glued to the top of the plastic floor unit and the interior parts are attached to it. A moulded corridor partition and individual compartment walls are provided. The couchettes are individual mouldings which can be attached to the compartment walls in either open or closed position. There are six beds to each compartment and the fitting of these is probably the most time-consuming part of the construction.

The windows, with their 'chromed' frames are individual mouldings, those for the toilets having realistically obscured glass. End vestibule doors, buffers and jumper cables are all ready-coloured

**Below: The Mougel Vu B10 C10 couchette vehicle.**

separate mouldings. Standard continental couplers, of pressed metal, are supplied. The bogies require careful assembly, but a little care is rewarded with fully operating suspension. The bogie parts are assembled with several small screws and those which form the pivots for the axleboxes must be treated with special care to avoid splitting the mountings. Main and secondary coil springs are provided, and the secondary suspension actually works, to give a very smooth-running model. All lettering is in the form of rub-on transfers, the only disappointing feature being the use of self-adhesive tape for the green roof band. The model is accurately dimensioned, scale length, and matches well with the Jouef Corail stock. It is not a cheap kit, but it is a delight to build and provides a good looking finished coach.

**Lee Town: GMC Astro truck kit**
In the United States, cast white metal is not a popular material for model railway kits, but it is used for a number of road vehicle kits, many of them to recognised railway scales. The Lee Town range in HO scale includes a variety of American truck types dating from the 1930s to the present day. The example shown here is a modern GMC Astro 3-axle tractor unit with sleeper cab and 16-wheel 'lowboy' trailer.

The kit comprises white metal parts for the tractor and trailer, with plastic wheels, rubber tyres and steel axles. The cast parts are commendably flash-free and assembly is quite straightforward. The inclusion of GMC logo transfers and moulded plastic windows (not vac-formed) are nice touches and the price not significantly higher than similar British models.

**Shinsei: Peterbilt with dump trailer**
This range of North American truck models marketed in the 'HO Haulers' banner consists of several truck/trailer combinations in HO scale. These are fully assembled and painted diecast models produced in Hong Kong. The wheels and tyres will need some attention before they satisfy serious modellers, and the self-adhesive striping on my example is crude and not very convincing. As a reasonably priced 'toy shop' model they form a useful basis for detailing as background on a modern layout.

**Jordan: 1920 Fordson tractor**
Old American road vehicles are featured in the Jordan range of plastic kits to HO scale. The little Fordson tractor is a delightful and inexpensive kit which requires careful assembly and handling because some of the parts are incredibly fine and fragile. Tweezers and good eyesight are essential for assembly of the smaller components. The model illustrated has solid tyres as used on the industrial version, but an agricultural type is also available.

**Juneco: Canadian National wood caboose**
The Canadian manufacturer, Juneco, has produced a number of interesting 'craftsman' kits in HO scale, based on Canadian prototypes. The term 'craftsman' suggests that these kits are aimed at the more experienced modeller, and this

**Below: Road vehicles by Lee Town, Jordan and Shinsei.**

is certainly true although a reasonably proficient modeller will find no difficulties if he follows the instructions carefully. The kit consists of milled basswood in various sizes for body parts, cast metal detail parts, and comprehensive instructions. Some measuring and cutting out of the basswood components is necessary, but this is simply accomplished with a sharp craft knife and steel rule. Impact adhesive is ideal for assembly of the wood parts, and for securing the castings, such as doors and windows.

Wire for handrails and other fittings is included, together with a set of the excellent CDS rub-on transfers. As is normal practice with kits of this type, trucks (bogies), and couplers are not included. The example illustrated runs on a pair of appropriate Lindberg trucks. The finished model is a very pleasant example of a typical wood-sheathed caboose from the 'steam' era, the only reservations concern the quality of some of the cast parts.

**Anbrico: GWR streamlined railcar**

This cast white metal kit in 4mm scale is a model of the steamlined 'Flying banana' railcars introduced by the Great Western Railway during the 1930s. It represents a car in the number series 5-16 in original condition with the full steamlined skirting intact. The castings are of very good quality and the kit is cleverly designed to minimise the number of individual parts. Assembly is therefore straightforward, and with a little care, a very good model will result.

The sides are cast in two halves with join disguised around the central door. Care taken to ensure a perfect join here will be well rewarded. The fit of the ends and floor provides no real problems, a minimal amount of filler being required to completely conceal the join lines. Cast interior partitions and seats are provided. The bogies are castings, supplied with wheels and the model is designed to be motorised with the little Tenshodo 'spud' bogie, or a K's motor. The Tenshodo bogie is secured in place with its own mounting bracket and is completely concealed below floor level. The wheels are hidden by the side skirting, and therefore bogie sideframes are not supplied. BR modellers may find this a little disappointing since the skirting over the bogies had been removed by the time of Nationalisation.

This is a splendid and unusual kit, which builds very nicely. The only real headache is the glazing of the curved cab ends, and this is probably best tackled from the outside with individual glazing pieces carefully cut to shape.

**Right: The Juneco Canadian National caboose.**

**Below: The prototype of the Anbrico model, in original condition.**

# Datafile 2

# Canadian Pacific Railway 'Royal Hudson' 4-6-4

Thirty streamlined 'Hudson' 4-6-4 locomotives, designed by H. B. Bowen, Chief Mechanical Engineer of the Canadian Pacific Railway and built by Montreal Locomotive Works, were delivered during 1937. They were numbered 2820-49 following an earlier batch of mechanically similar 'Hudsons' Nos 2803-19. The new locomotives were intended for use on heavy trans-continental passenger and freight trains. They were designed to run at sustained high speeds for up to 800 miles without changing engines.

The semi-streamlined styling was similar to that used on the earlier 4-4-4 locomotives and disposed of the many projecting parts, external headlights and plumbing which had been a feature of North American locomotives. The chimney was set in a streamlined fairing, there was no dome, a small safety valve cowling, and the obligatory headlight was moved to the centre of the smokebox front. The stylish livery included tuscan red panels on the tender, cab and footplate valance, and a planished steel boiler. Mechanical stokers and air reversers were fitted.

Five of the locomotives, Nos 2838-42 were fitted with a booster to increase the tractive effort and these were followed by a further batch taking the total to 65, of which the last five were equipped for oil-burning. During 1949-50 a further 16 were converted to burn oil. This final batch were for service on the steeply graded section of the trans-continental route — between Revelstoke and Vancouver. Shortly after delivery No 2850 was called upon to haul the Royal train during the 1939 tour of Canada by King George VI and Queen Elizabeth. For this tour it was specially finished in Royal blue and silver livery, and so successfully did it prove its capacity for sustained running that it received official Royal approval. From henceforth, the locomotives were known as 'Royal Hudsons' and carried a cast crown emblem on the footplate valance. Despite its appearance, the chimney was a single chimney equipped with a cowl which could be raised to deflect the blast in tunnels. Most of the class were later fitted with a more conventional chimney.

**Below: 'Royal Hudson' No 2850 in the blue and grey Royal Train livery.** *Ian Allan Library*

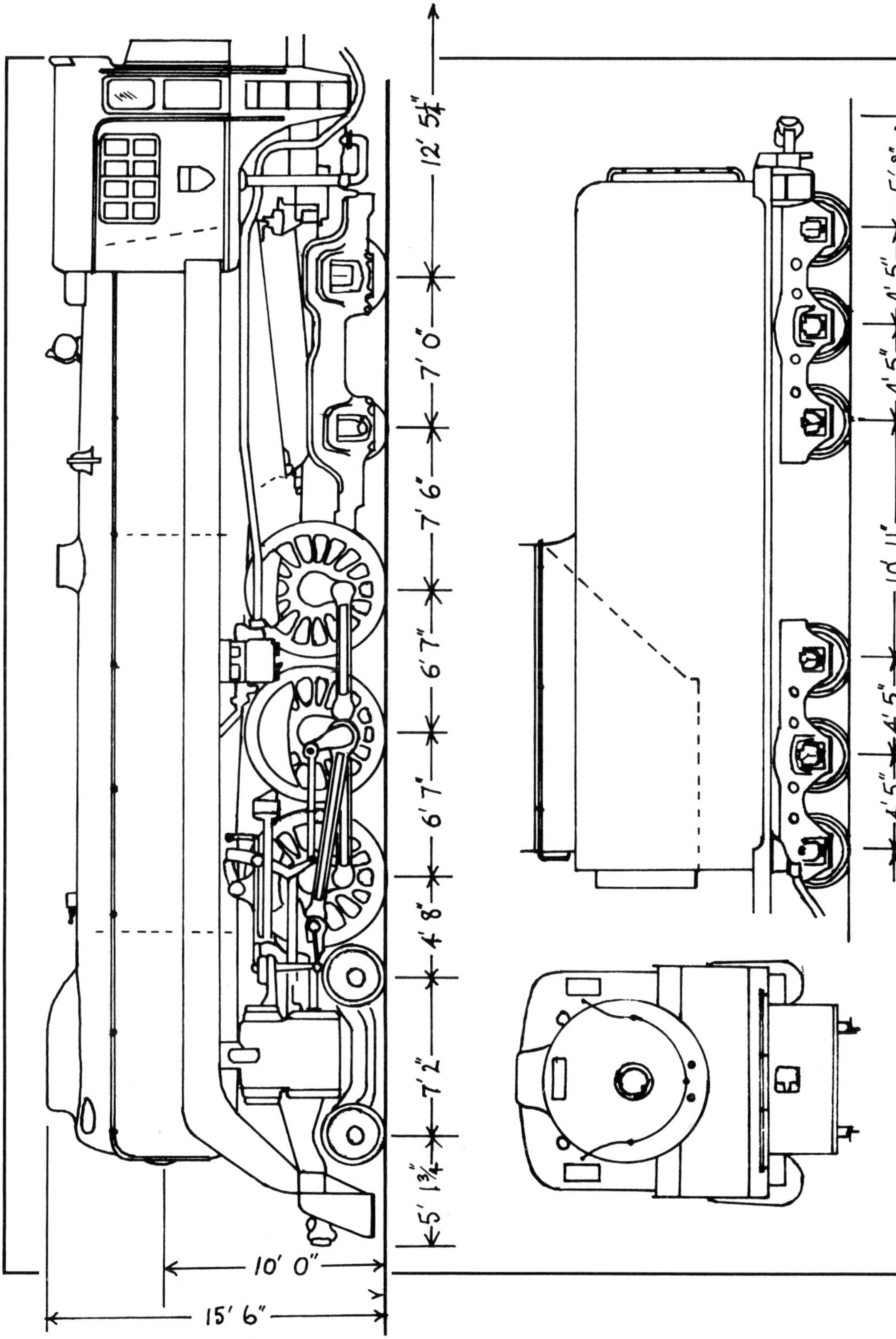


*Drawing 3.5mm:1ft scale*

2852
2852
CANADIAN PACIFIC

2860
2860
BRITISH COLUMBIA
CANADA

**Above left: The standard CPR maroon livery applied to No 2852. Not all examples had the number board on the chimney.** *Canadian Pacific*

**Left: Preserved 'Royal Hudson' No 2860 wears a compromise livery of CPR maroon embellished with additional lettering and crests. It is here seen working north from Vancouver with an excursion to Squamish.** *D. A. Anderson*

**Above: The preserved 'Royal Hudson' No 2860 seen in its first year of operation on the British Columbia Railway, leaving North Vancouver.** *J. G. Greenall*

Two members of the class are preserved in working order, No 2839 on the Southern Railway in the USA and No 2860 by the Provincial Government of British Columbia.

**Data:**

*Cylinders:* 22in dia by 30in stroke
*Boiler pressure:* 275lb per sq in
*Tractive effort:* 45,000lb
57,000lb with booster
*Wheelbase:*
Driving: 13ft 2in
Engine: 39ft 6in
*Engine/Tender:* 80ft $6\frac{1}{4}$in
*Firebox:* 10ft 11in long × 7ft 5in wide
*Grate area:* 80.8 sq ft
*Weight (with booster)*
on driving wheels: 83tons 6cwt
total engine/tender: 294tons 8cwt

# A modern engineers' train

*Chris Leigh*

Modellers seldom seem to pay much attention to engineer's or departmental vehicles, possibly because there have been few proprietary models, apart from the odd short-lived crane such as the Airfix Booth Rodley or the little Tri-ang hand crane. These days the BR departmental fleet is a curious mixture of old vehicles, some going back to the 1920s and beyond, with some of the latest equipment and sophisticated technology. For the modeller these older vehicles may be of interest, if only to provide the modern-image modeller with an excuse to run something a bit antiquated on his layout. Many of the modern machines, tampers, ballast cleaners and the like are probably too complex to be worth the average modeller's time in attempting to model them. The modelling possibilities of a short engineers' train were recently brought to my attention again by events on the local Western Region branch from West Drayton to Staines West. Following the running of the last train on 24 January 1981 I had determined to keep a record of the track-lifting operations on the branch to complete my file of pictures on the history of the line.

Once the track-lifting commenced it was as if the work was being done by ghosts, with work progressing but never a train to be seen. Vigilance paid off, and within a few days I had seen my 'ghost' — a most curious train indeed. There was no locomotive, the short train of two wagons and

**Below: Plasser & Theurer GPC-72 crane No 81509 approaches the site of Yeoveney halt with the Staines branch demolition train in March 1981. Note the oxygen and acetylene cylinders visible to the left of the jib.** *Chris Leigh*

**Right: Sleeping and mess van No DB 975411, formerly a 'Fruit D' van, working in the company of the Didcot-based Plasser crane.** *Chris Leigh*

a mess van being worked to the site by a modern self-propelled crane. In this article I shall describe the vehicles which formed the train. They could of course, be hauled by a conventional locomotive, and when running on a main line they certainly would be so hauled. However, I set out to build a working model of the crane too. It is not yet finished but I have included a description of the work done so far.

**The mess van**

It was this vehicle which first set my mind working on the modelling project, when I realised that it would be a fairly straightforward conversion job. The prototype, No DB 975411, was converted from a WR passenger fruit van of the same type as the Hornby-Dublo (now Wrenn) model. It was provided with windows in each end and both sides and fitted with lockers on the

*Drawing 4mm:1ft scale*

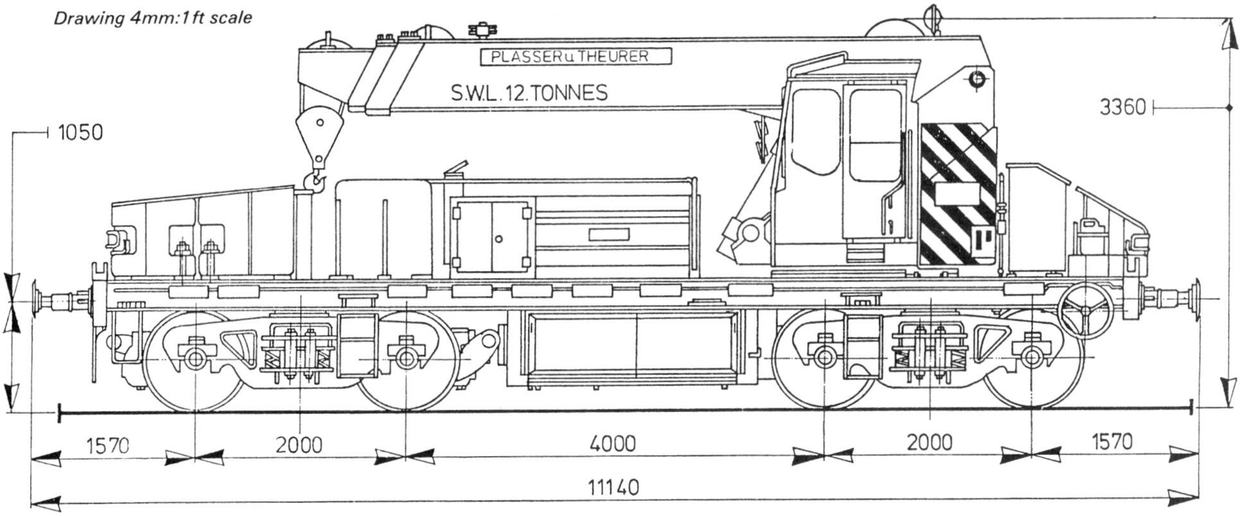

**Above: The converted tube wagon, glimpsed through the undergrowth on a misty March morning. Most of the original lettering was still visible on this side.** *Chris Leigh*

underframe, but was otherwise little altered. The vehicle was originally W3465W (built Swindon 1955) and is a one-off conversion carried out at Cardiff Cathays in 1974. It was then numbered KDB 975382 and used by the S&T Dept at Reading.

Examination of the Wrenn model revealed one or two other problems in that, while the body is a well-detailed plastic moulding, the underframe is a mazac casting with most of the detail omitted. I commenced work on the body by separating it from the chassis and putting the single self-tapping screw aside for re-use. I then marked in the position of the windows with a steel rule and scriber using the planks on the model as a guide to correct positioning. The corners of each window aperture were then drilled with a $^1/_{32}$in drill hand-held in a pin chuck, and the window centres drilled out $^1/_8$in dia with a hand drill. When holding the body in a vice it is advisable to cushion the jaws with something soft to prevent damage to the delicate detail on the moulding. The window apertures were then filed out to shape.

At this stage I found it best to get all drilling and filing finished as the moulding produces a very soft, clinging dust. I therefore drilled and filed out the 'webs' within the steps under each door, removed the centre steps completely, and removed all the roof-top vents and lamp tops, leaving only the rain strips intact. The vent positions, but not the lamps, were then drilled through $^1/_{16}$in dia to take new torpedo vents. The body shell was next thoroughly washed in warm water with an old toothbrush to remove all the dust, and set aside to dry.

Attention then turned to the underframe. This has all the truss-rods and Morton brake gear omitted and I decided from the outset that these would have to go on. I began by cutting off the buffers, cleaning up the buffer beam and drilling new buffer holes $^1/_{16}$in dia. The correct pattern GWR large wagon/van buffers are available in the ABS Models range and these were secured in place with five minute epoxy. I cut off the two small brake levers on the corners of the underframe, but left the centrally placed 'V' hangers as these would be hidden by the lockers. Also at this stage the spoked plastic wheelsets were eased out of the pressed metal axle-bearing plates. I fitted Jackson wheels of the three-hole disc type, as on the prototype mess van, slight filing of the axle ends being necessary in order to obtain satisfactory free-running of the wheels.

The fitting of the various underframe parts improved the model beyond my expectations and did not prove as difficult as I had imagined. A 4mm scale drawing of the Fruit D appears in *A History of GWR Wagons-Vol 2* published by David & Charles. This provided a useful guide to the layout of the various rods and levers which are not readily discernible from photographs. I began by making up the truss-rod unit. I had planned to use small 'L' section brass and to attach it direct to the mazac underframe using epoxy adhesive. However, suitable brass was not readily obtainable locally so I opted for very small 'L' section Plastruct strip.

A baseplate of 30thou styrene sheet 55mm by 20mm was cut out and a hole made in the centre to clear the vacuum cylinder and mounting screw on the underside of the mazac chassis. This plate was to provide a false floor to which the truss rods would be attached and some care was necessary to ensure that it fitted easily in the correct location on the chassis. The positions of the four vertical truss-rod posts were then marked on the long edges of this false floor, and square notches were cut in the edge to take the posts. The four posts were cut from the Plastruct strip and secured in place with Plastruct solvent adhesive, making sure they remained upright. The truss rods, two pieces of the strip 78mm long were then cut. The bends were formed at the point where the rods attach to the posts, by cutting a tiny 'V' notch in one web of the 'L' section sufficient to enable it to bend without distortion. The trussrods were then secured to the posts and the edges of the false floor with solvent. For added strength I installed a couple of cross members to brace the truss rods apart. The finished unit was then secured to the underframe with Evo-Stik.

The brake gear consists of two 'V' hangers on each side with a single brake lever. I cannibalised a Ratio kit to obtain these parts, but suitable fittings can no doubt be obtained individually from one of the wagon kit and accessory manufacturers. The Ratio brake lever had to be bent slightly to fit in place below the right hand doors but otherwise the installation was quite straightforward. I then used pieces of plastic rod to link the 'V' hangers with the brake shoe pres-

**Below: A GPC-72 crane on the Eastern Region near Bishops Stortford. The shaping of the rear bodywork can be clearly seen.** *C. P. Hudson*

sings on the chassis. It struck me as rather odd that 20 years ago Hornby-Dublo had managed to produce wagons with brake shoes in line with the wheels, yet this is still apparently beyond most proprietary manufacturers.

The only other job was to add the two chassis-mounted lockers below the centre pairs of doors. These were made up from styrene sheet and glued in place against the unwanted 'V' hangers. Hinges and handles were added from tiny pieces of 10thou styrene sheet.

The prototype mess van is finished in a distinctive colour scheme of green with yellow ends. In order to obtain the very matt finish of the prototype I airbrushed the body using Gloy dmu green mixed with a drop of matt white to obtain

**Above: Points to note in this view are the arrangement of lighting on the ends and the solebar, and the layout of the roping. This was an SR-based crane seen working at Staines.** *Chris Leigh*

the required shade. The ends and underframe locker boxes were painted with two coats of signal yellow, and the underframe in matt black.

The lettering is probably the least satisfactory aspect of the model but I was unable to find an alternative to hand painting, due to the very small size of the lettering. So, armed with the knowledge that most of the lettering on the prototype was very worn and faint (and could therefore be the same on the model!) I set to work with white paint and a No 00 brush. Reading from the left hand end, the wording on each side is laid out as follows:

| | | |
|---|---|---|
| DCE LONDON | SLEEPING | WB 18-0 |
| TO WORK WITH | & | |
| PLASSER CRANE | MESS VAN | |
| 81509 | | |
| DB 975411 | | |

I took the view that if it looked too terrible I could brush some thinned green over it to produce the 'worn away' effect of the original. The finishing touch was the addition of a Springside tail lamp, as this vehicle was serving as the brake van in the train.

**The 'runner'**

Having decided to model the whole train, and not just the mess van I was faced with a rather more problematic project than the simple conversion job. The Plasser self-propelled crane has a telescopic jib and so does not require a 'runner' or match wagon on which to support the jib when in the travelling mode. However, crews on a job such as track-lifting need to carry certain tools such as crow bars, fishplate bolt spanners, and gas cylinders for oxy-acetylene cutting equipment. A converted BR 'TUBE' wagon was provided for carrying this sort of equipment, but I was unable to locate a suitable model on which to base a similar conversion. So there was no alternative but to scratch-build, and if you are going to start scratch-building wagons, an open merchandise vehicle of this sort is an easy first project.

The vehicle in question was No DB 732251, classified under TOPS code ZDV, a 22$\frac{1}{2}$ton 'TUBE' converted for departmental use. The prototype was a BR Standard version of the LMS tube wagon, with corrugated steel ends and five-plank wooden body. It was little changed from original condition, apart from the removal of the doors and the fitting of tubular steps and handrails.

I began by cutting a floor of styrene sheet 32mm by 126mm and scoring the planking on the upper surface, making sure that this did not distort the floor. The solebars were cut from suitable section brass strip and glued in place with Evo-Stik using styrene cross members to ensure correct spacing. Axleguards for 'modern' stock seem hard to find among the various suppliers of model parts so I eventually settled upon a scrapped Airfix Esso tank wagon kit and cannibalised it. I kept each axleguard intact with the section of solebar immediately above it and filed the detail off the face of the solebar moulding until left with a 'tongue' which fitted behind the new brass solebar. Each axlebox was carefully drilled to accept a Peco bearing cup and the axleguards and Jackson wheelsets were then installed on the chassis. I had a BR diagram

**Below: Plasser crane No 81511, also seen at Staines on the Southern Region. The lights are switched on for work on a dreary January afternoon. Note the rear view of the crane body, the off-set winding mechanism and the complex body shape.** *Chris Leigh*

which showed the axle centres as 18ft 6in so I set them at this spacing despite the fact that some other publications show 17ft 6in as the measurement.

Once the axleboxes had set firmly, I started work on the body which consists of 30 thou styrene sheet, scored for planking and secured in place around the edges of the floor. The four side panels measure 59mm by 12mm, and the ends 12mm by 32mm. Before fitting the ends it is necessary to cover them with suitable currugated material. I used some basswood of American manufacture, but Slaters Plastikard or foil strip would be equally suitable. Once the ends were fitted, the side pieces were glued in place and left to set after making sure everything was square.

Body detailing commenced with the 'L' section stanchions on the outside of each end. These were 15mm lengths of the same Plastruct strip used for the mess van underframe. They are inset 8mm from the sides so they fall just inside the buffers. The body strapping was all from a Scalelink etched rivet fret No F16, using the thinnest strips for the diagonals and the next thicker ones for the verticals. The vertical strips were glued in place first, taking care to avoid glue spreading out from underneath the strips. Before fitting the outer diagonal strips, the angled corner plates were cut from paper, folded around the corners and glued in place. These are a very dis-

tinctive feature, particularly in view of the way this wagon is painted.

A single strip of styrene sheet 2mm high was installed across the foot of each door opening. On the prototype there appears to be one plank across each door, presumably to prevent tools laid on the floor from rolling out. The step and handrail units were made up from soft wire using a simple jig. I cut a strip of card to the internal width of the steps (7mm) and glued this to a card base. When dry I cut slots in the card strip at the location of each step and just wide enough to hold the wire steps. The wire frame was then folded around the outside of the card strip, individual wire steps were pressed into the slots, and the whole thing soldered up.

The 'TUBE' wagon has a rather naked underframe so it is important to include such details as there are, and these comprise brake shoes and brake rigging. I made up the buffer beams from two layers of styrene sheet, drilled and fitted with the ABS buffers as used on the mess van. These are not really quite right for this vehicle, but in the absence of anything better, they look reasonable. For the brake shoes and 'V' hangers I returned to the scrapped Airfix Esso tanker and carefully removed the appropriate parts. I cut through the chassis, cutting and filing off various bits until I was left with four similar chassis sections, each with a pair of brake shoes attached. These were then carefully fitted around the wheels and secured to the styrene floor with Plastruct solvent, taking care that none of the shoes was rubbing on a wheel. The 'V' hangers and vac cylinders were also cut from the Airfix chassis and secured in place on the centreline below the doors. All that remained was to add brake rigging from plastic rod, in a configuration roughly the same as was visible in photographs.

The body was given two coats of BR bauxite and the floor two coats of matt dark earth. I then picked out random planks in slightly darkened bauxite, as on the prototype. The ends and the angled corner plates were painted in signal yellow and the underframe in matt black, before being given the treatment with some dirty turps. Lettering once again required hand painted work. The finished model is very light and may yet require the addition of some small lead strips under the floor. However, for the moment I have decided to experiment with using the load to provide weight. The gas cylinders were made up from suitable pieces of brass rod turned to shape in the chuck of an electric drill. Tools were from Cooper Craft and pieces of brass wire, and rail chairs from Springside. A great deal of time and effort can be put into the detailing of the load, tools, etc and it is rewarded with an interesting and rather 'different' model.

**The rail wagon**

Although a few complete track sections were lifted during the operations which I watched, these were merely moved further up the line and broken up on site. Only the rails were recovered,

**Views of the model crane and its accompanying vehicles. One or two detailing jobs on the crane were still to be done when these photographs were taken.**

and subsequently sleepers and chairs were left in the ballast. The rails were loaded on to a bogie bolster wagon and it usually took about two days, work to complete the load and propel it up the branch to where it was exchanged for an empty wagon. Thus, a number of bogie bolsters, both vacuum-braked and unfitted types, were used.

For the model I took the easy way out and used the Palitoy Mainline bogie bolster virtually without modification. I use Peco couplings, so these had to be changed, and I dirtied the model and added a few pieces of wooden packing, some lengths of bullhead rail painted in rust brown and chains to complete the job.

**The Plasser Crane**

Track-lifting on the Staines branch commenced on 29 January 1981 and was still in progress at the end of March. The crane and vehicles featured here were only in use between 24 February and 6 March. The rest of the work was done by a much older diesel crane with a 'runner' and mess van bearing Great Western Railway Swindon Works builder's plates. This crane also hauled its own train to the site, but did so much less impressively at walking pace and with the jib partly raised. On the other hand, it was the neat and business-like appearance of the Plasser crane and its short train which had first interested me in the idea of modelling it.

The Plasser GPC-72 cranes were introduced during 1978 and a total of 30 was built, a further 14 very similar machines being supplied by Cowans Sheldon. Features of the design include a telescopic jib which can be stowed within the 39ft overall length of the unit when travelling, and a very small tail overhang on the crane body so that it does not foul adjacent tracks when working 'over the side'. The crane is capable of a self-propelled maximum speed of around 15mph and weighs 86 tonnes.

I wanted my crane model to fulfil certain functions, and particularly to be capable of hauling its train, and of being posed in a variety of positions with the main parts functioning but without sacrificing scale appearance. In other words, the mechanism had to fit within the very confined space available, in a model about 6in long, and there must be no great winding handles or other compromises to make it work.

The first problem was easily overcome. I had recently purchased an Anbrico GWR railcar which utilises a 26mm wheelbase Tenshodo motor bogie. This is quite the neatest motor bogie I have ever seen. It is smooth running and quiet at low speeds, and its mechanism fits completely below floor level. At a scale 6ft 6in wheelbase it is only a 'gnats-whisker' away from the 2m wheelbase of the Plasser crane bogie, so it formed the obvious choice for the model. I decided to build the main components, the frame, floor, crane jib and body out of soldered brass and to use styrene sheet for the rest of the construction.

The jib is made up from three pieces of rectangular section brass tube as sold on the K&S Metal displays in many model shops. I selected three pieces of approximately the correct dimensions, each one being a sliding fit inside the others. However, in the vertical dimension they were not a close fit and had to be packed with styrene to suit the correct measurements. The actual operation of the jib has proved to be a real teaser, since I wanted a degree of prototypical operation. A length of fine fishing line joins each pair of jib sections, inside the hollow tube, and prevents them from being over extended. For the moment they are simply hand operated, various winding systems and spring arrangements having been tried unsuccessfully.

The base of the crane body was cut from brass sheet and the two triangular bracket pieces were soldered to it. These formed the main structural components of the crane. The bracket pieces were drilled $\frac{1}{16}$in in the top corner for the jib pivot, and the raised boss was similarly drilled for the hydraulic ram mounting. The main jib section was installed next, the pivot being a piece of brass rod soldered in place and forming a tight fit so that the jib would remain in any position without collapsing.

The hydraulic ram consists of a piece of $\frac{1}{8}$in dia nickel silver rod sliding in a piece of $\frac{1}{8}$in inside diameter brass tube. At its lower end the tube is pivotted to the crane superstructure, while the upper end of the nickel silver rod is pivotted to the jib bracing piece. The latter is cut from the same tube as the jib section, and filed to the correct tapered shape. This was soldered in place and the two parts of the hydraulic ram slipped together. The crane structure was then attached to the chassis, using an 8BA bolt to provide the pivot.

The cab is assembled from styrene sheet, with the sides and front panel formed of glazing material overlaid with 10thou thick styrene sheet to give a flush glazed appearance. It was essential to include a seat and operator. The rest of the body is also styrene, the curved back being produced from 10thou over suitable formers. The roof is formed from two layers of styrene sheet, filed to the correct shamfered profile. Handrails were added from thin brass wire, and the cab door is a separate fitting built up from 10thou styrene overlaid on the glazing material. The equipment housing which occupies the opposite side of the crane body from the cab was made up from styrene sheet, the top being drilled No 68 to take some strips of thread which represent the flexible connections to the jib.

All the equipment boxes which form the superstructure, including the end sections with angled corners and sloping tops, were fabricated from styrene sheet. The cut away sections are particularly important in capturing the character of the vehicle. Those at the corners house movable high intensity lights, while the side cut outs in the rearmost section contain large water cans. The buffer beams are laminated from a strip of 30thou styrene overlaid on a strip of 10thou, the latter having the lifting rings drilled No 68. These fit neatly in the angled corners of the body sections. The buffer beams were painted matt yellow, and the black chevrons added with a Rotring drawing pen before any further detailing was done. The buffers are the correct Oleo pattern, taken from an MTK dmu kit, for which they were incorrect. Hoses and lamp brackets were added from wire, and a screw coupling was fitted to the front buffer beam.

The bogie sideframes were cut from brass sheet, drilled and filed to shape. Those for the motor bogie were glued to the Tenshodo mounting bracket with Evo-Stik. The trailing bogie was assembled with a brass bolster, drilled and attached to the chassis with an 8BA bolt. This was soldered in place to prevent it working loose. Wheels for the trailing bogie proved a problem, since those on the motor bogie are only some 10mm in diameter, with fine RP-25 flanges. British wheels appeared very large in comparison, so I settled upon a set of North American coach wheels. The rest of the bogie sideframe detail is mainly scrap-box material, including axleboxes (light lenses from a plastic kit) and springs (sections of thread from discarded K's nylon screws).

Final detailing of the model still remains to be carried out, and at present the roping has been temporarily installed. The rope is nylon fishing line. The winding gear is mounted on the side of the main jib section and the rope runs to a pulley arrangement at the end of this section. From here it passes through eyes on the top outer ends of the other two jib sections. At the extreme end of the jib, the rope passes through a guide which takes it down the side of the jib, and from there it is carried around the pulley on the lifting hook and its free end is attached inside the hollow end of the jib. The hook, roping eyes and temporary pulley arrangement are all made up from styrene, but the winding gear will be replaced with a working arrangement, turned up in the drill chuck. I provided a 45ft section of SMP bullhead track, slung from chains for a suitable load, but the underframe must be weighted to compensate for the weight of the jib when working over the side.

The model was given three coats of Humbrol matt yellow, all the bodywork, the jib, and underframe gear between the bogies being standard BR departmental yellow. The chassis, solebars, floor and bogies are matt black. Buffer stocks and the backs of buffer heads are matt orange, and the buffer faces are burnished metal. After the solebars had been painted strips of white 20thou styrene were glued in place to represent the row of fluorescent lights carried by the prototype. The bogie steps and handrails are painted white.

A distinctive feature of the real crane is the large amount of lettering which it carries, and here I reluctantly had to turn once more to hand lettering. Most of the signs were lettered with a Rotring pen on white paper and glued in place, but the red lettering on the cab front and jib, and the BR logos, were brush painted directly on to the model. The black chevrons on the back of the crane body were drawn on some yellow-painted paper using the Rotring pen. The large lettering 'WMG Plasser Theurer' was painted in red and black on white paper, and the chevron piece was then cut out and glued in place over the lettered sheet.

The crane, with its short train makes a most unusual sight and so far it has created a great deal of interest wherever it goes.

# Great Western Railway stables at Shipton

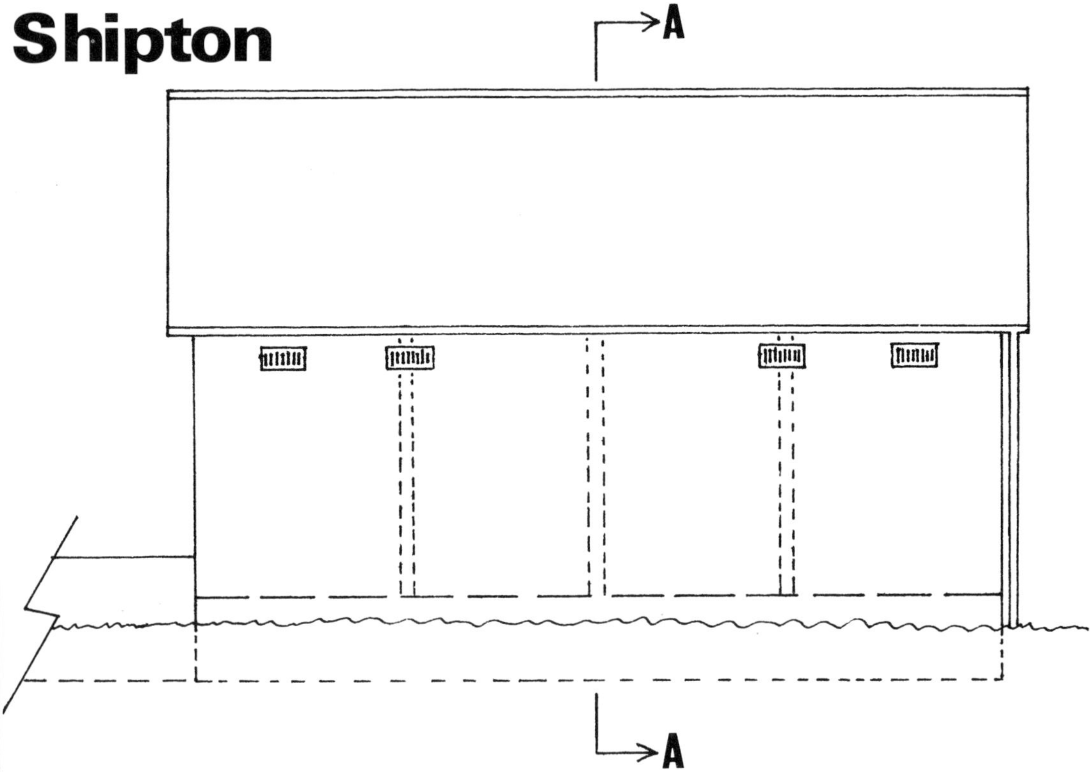


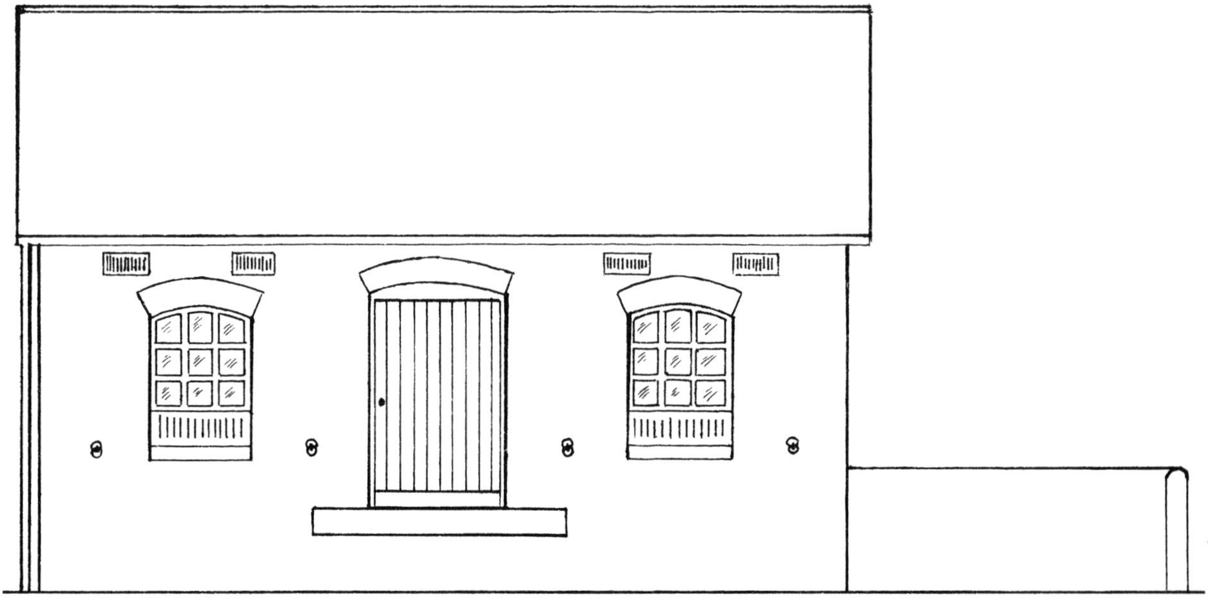

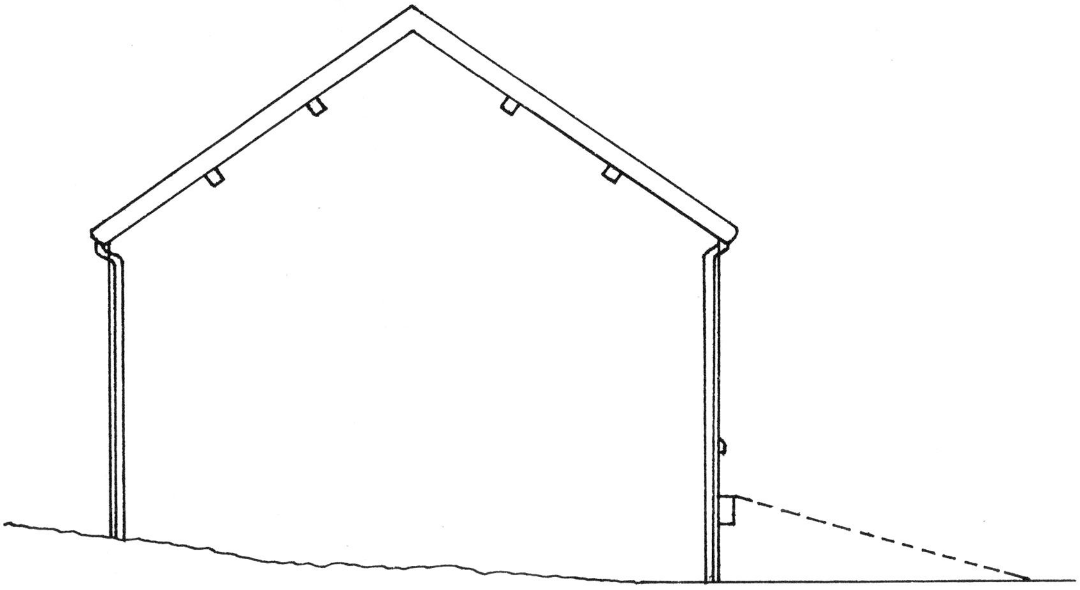

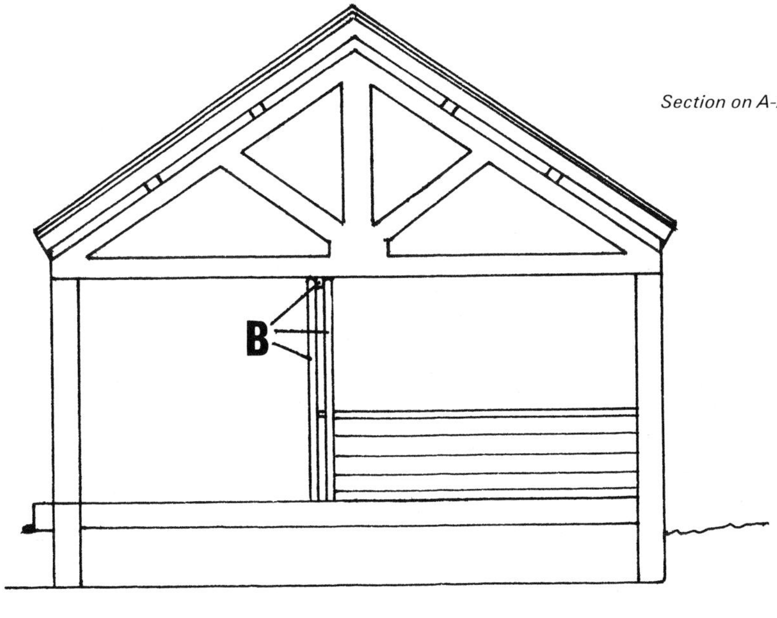


*Section on A-A*

Before the advent of the motor lorry, horses were the mainstay of local goods delivery services. The GWR operated extensive cartage services between country station goods yards and local towns, and many such goods yards were provided with stables. From the final years of the 19th century standardised building designs were introduced by the Great Western and although individual designs differed to suit their location, they made use of standardised components. Considerable economies of scale were thus possible when large quantities of identical doors, windows and fittings could be purchased. Design and construction could also be simplified where components were interchangeable.

The stable block at Shipton for Burford on the Cotswold line is a pretty little structure built of standard GWR parts. It was still standing in 1981 although sadly disused and derelict. It is built of dark blue engineers' bricks, in English bond, and has a roof of grey slates. The floor is raised above the surrounding ground level, probably due to problems with water draining off the field which rises behind it. There must have been a ramp to give access to the door, and on the drawing I have indicated this with a dotted line. Sliding ventilators were provided in the front and back walls, and also below the windows and these were standard GWR fittings. Note, too, the four iron hitching rings on the front wall. The front corners of the structure featured the rounded 'bullnose' bricks so beloved of the Great Western, and these stop short, twelve courses from the top, the final courses being of ordinary bricks.

The floor is timber and the interior is equipped with four stalls separated by 3ft high timber partitions as shown in the section drawing. The items marked 'B' at the end of each partition consist of vertical posts of bullhead rail bolted to a horizontal bridge rail fixed upside down on the underside of the roof trusses. Metal feed baskets were hung on the inside of the rear wall. The low-walled area at the right-hand end was, of course, a compound for 'manure' and the lower part of the end wall within the compound was cement rendered to simplify cleaning.

This is the sort of small structure which could easily be fitted into a model goods yard and would be easy to super-detail. In many cases, when motor lorries replaced the horses, the stables were converted into garages, simply by providing large doors in one end.

**Right: A glimpse inside the Shipton stables showing arrangement of stalls and roof truss.** *Chris Leigh*

**Below: Shipton stables seen in 1980. Note the ventilators and the tethering rings.** *Chris Leigh*

# Lillooet

## - a prototype for the modeller

*Chris Leigh*

Photographs by the author unless otherwise shown

In recent years many modellers have forsaken the idea of producing an imaginary location for their layout, and have turned their attentions to finding a prototype location which suited their modelling interests. The many rail closures of the 1960s probably added extra impetus to this trend, as modellers saw their favourite locations disappearing and sought to recreate them in miniature. A marvellous variety of different approaches were, and still are, evident covering everything from the severely compressed and 'loosely based on such and such' approach, to the layout which is precise to an exact moment in time.

In North America, where large layout spaces are often available, the emphasis tends to be on grand model railroad schemes where the imagination runs riot and a breath-taking array of tracks and scenery is the result. Such layouts are splendid for viewing and operating but the amount of time and space, not to mention financial outlay, is seldom available to British modellers. Perhaps, when a British modeller with a preference for modelling specific prototype locations takes an interest in North American practice, a most interesting compromise in layout design ought to result. I hope so! Articles describing prototype locations which are particularly suitable for modelling have become a popular feature of the British model railway magazines. Indeed, even a few European locations have received similar treatment. My own layout, still in the early stages of development, is to have Lillooet as its main station, and this article looks at this all too rare example of a Canadian wayside station, though a model-maker's eyes.

**History**

I can't really recall how I, as a dedicated GWR/SR enthusiast, first became interested in North American modelling, but I guess it was probably a result of the disparity in quality between British and American products of some 15 years ago. In the days when Trix, Hornby and Tri-ang all had different wheel standards and incompatible couplings there was something very attractive about the degree of standardisation among American products. More recently my dormant interest in North American modelling began to flourish with the purchase of some rolling stock, followed in 1976 by a visit to western Canada. The choice of Lillooet as a suitable prototype for modelling began when I saw a couple of photographs of its pretty timber station building. With a 19ft by 9ft loft space available and an ever-increasing collection of Canadian freight cars the first steps in reproducing Lillooet in HO scale were taken.

The town of Lillooet (pronounce it as three distinct syllables) is situated 157 miles north of Vancouver in British Columbia, Canada. The soft-sounding Indian name betrays its ethnic origins, and it was not until the coming of the railway in 1921 that Lillooet and its surroundings began to be opened up to the outside world. In the 19th century it had gained some notoriety when gold was discovered in the surrounding hills, and later it became the starting point of the 'Caribou Highway', a trail by which pioneers and prospectors made their way north. In recent years its importance has ebbed away again. The main highway leads east from the town towards Cache Creek and Lytton and central BC, but the journey south to Vancouver still entails either a long drive over dirt roads which are impassable in winter, or a five hour rail journey.

Lillooet is served by the British Columbia Railway, formerly the Pacific Great Eastern, which links North Vancouver with communities in central and northern BC as far as Fort Nelson, some 250 miles from the Yukon border. If there is ever a rail link between the USA and Alaska, the BCR will form a large section of it. Construction of the railway was slow and piecemeal. The section from Squamish through Lillooet to Quesnel opened in 1921, but it was not until 1956 that the Squamish-North Vancouver section was completed. Fort Nelson was reached in 1972, and today some branch lines are still under construction as the railway adapts to the transport needs of a developing province.

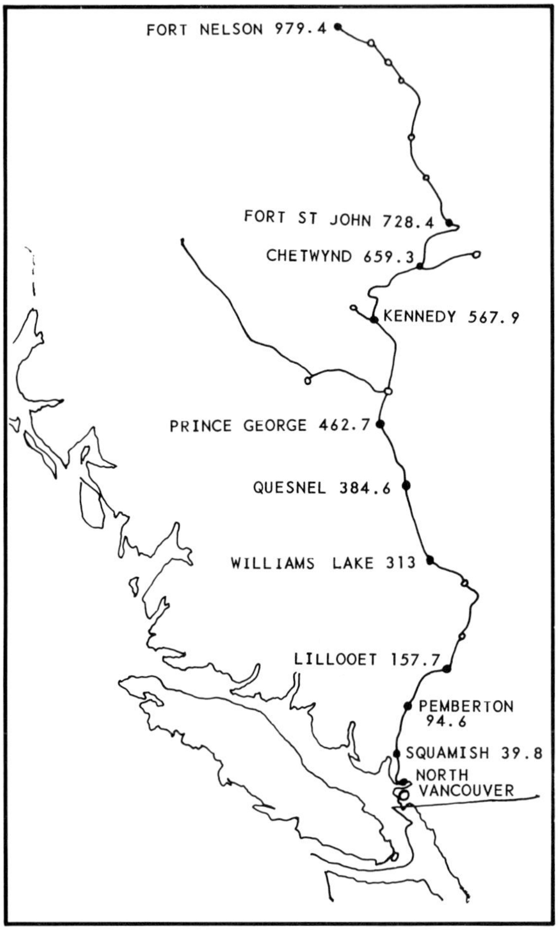


**Geography**

The BCR main line is a steeply graded single track, of over 1,000 route miles. It traverses the rugged country of the Coast Mountains with long stretches of 1 in 50 gradients, passing through the Cheakamus canyon and following the shores of Anderson and Seton lakes for many miles before emerging into the Fraser valley at Lillooet. Here, the benchlands above the river form a fertile growing area, but the countryside is otherwise dry with sage brush and scrubby trees on the hills. Lillooet itself occupies the lower slopes of the hills on the west bank of the Fraser river. It is a hot, dusty place where every moving vehicle leaves a white dust-cloud behind it. While I was there, the temperature hit 95 degrees and the sun beat down out of a deep blue sky. The road from Vancouver via Squamish becomes the main street of Lillooet and parallels the railway. The station approach is a short dirt road on the right and immediately beyond it the highway to Lytton diverges to the right. It crosses the railway on an unprotected level crossing, newly equipped with warning lights, and descends steeply to cross the Fraser on a new concrete bridge. This has replaced a much more interesting timber suspension bridge which was restricted to use by one vehicle at a time.

**Track plan**

The station building, known as the passenger depot in Canadian terminology, is situated on the west side of the main line and has a short rail-level gravel platform. North of the station a trailing turnout provides access to two sidings, one serving an oil terminal and the other passing close behind the station building. On the other side of the main line is a long passing loop with turnouts forming several shorter loops and giving access to the yard tracks. The yard is formed in a 'wye' or triangle, a customary feature of Canadian railways which provides the facility for turning equipment such as snowploughs or groups of diesel locomotives coupled together. The tracks on the east side of the 'wye' are used for stabling engineer's equipment, including the fully equipped work trains with living accommodation, water tankers etc, which are necessary for work in remote areas.

The third side of the 'wye' contains servicing

facilities for locomotives and rolling stock. A prominent feature is the sand tower which delivers specially dried sand to the locomotives. Sanding is still used as the principle means of aiding adhesion on steep gradients and wet rails. Offices, mess rooms and workshops are provided in several single-storey timber cabins but all maintenance work is done in the open nowadays, although it is possible that Lillooet once had a locomotive shed. Running repairs to rolling stock can be carried out and lifting tackle is provided to enable freight cars to be lifted for emergency wheel changes. There is also a stabling area for the ubiquitous 'speeders' — sophisticated platelayers' trollies which run ahead of some trains to check for rockslides or to assist in changing points when trains have to cross at remote passing loops.

**Structures**

The main railway structure, and the centrepiece of my layout design, is the passenger depot building. It is a typical design from the early years of the present century, and similar to others on the original section of the BCR, particularly those at Quesnel and Williams Lake. It is built of timber, mainly faced with shiplapped planks or white finished shingles, and has a roof of red shingles. The woodwork is painted pale blue and white. An unloading platform for small trucks and the 'pick-ups' much used in western Canada is provided at one end of the building, while much of the structure is taken up with offices for operating staff. A door at the south end gives access to the booking office, which is a spartan little room with a bench seat and a 'Coke' machine. The latter is essential in view of the heat! When the weather is good, most passengers choose to wait outside and an hour before train time passengers start to gather and piles of packages are assembled on the platform.

On the opposite side of the line, north of the road crossing is a disused and overgrown freight platform, but otherwise railway structures are limited to an assortment of cabins, ancient and modern, alongside the yard tracks. The nearest major engineering feat is an impressive steel bridge over the Fraser, 3 miles north of the town. Most of the dwellings, and even the shops are timber-built, single storey structures, although there are one or two houses on Main Street in grander style, but still built of timber. There are only a handful of shops spread along the mile or so of Main Street — a couple of restaurants, general store, furniture, hairdresser, dentist, museum, drug store etc, and a tiny newspaper office.

**Traffic**

British Columbia Railway is primarily a heavy freight carrier which is in the business of opening up access to the natural wealth of the province. Its main traffic is in forest products and minerals, including logs, timber products, paper,

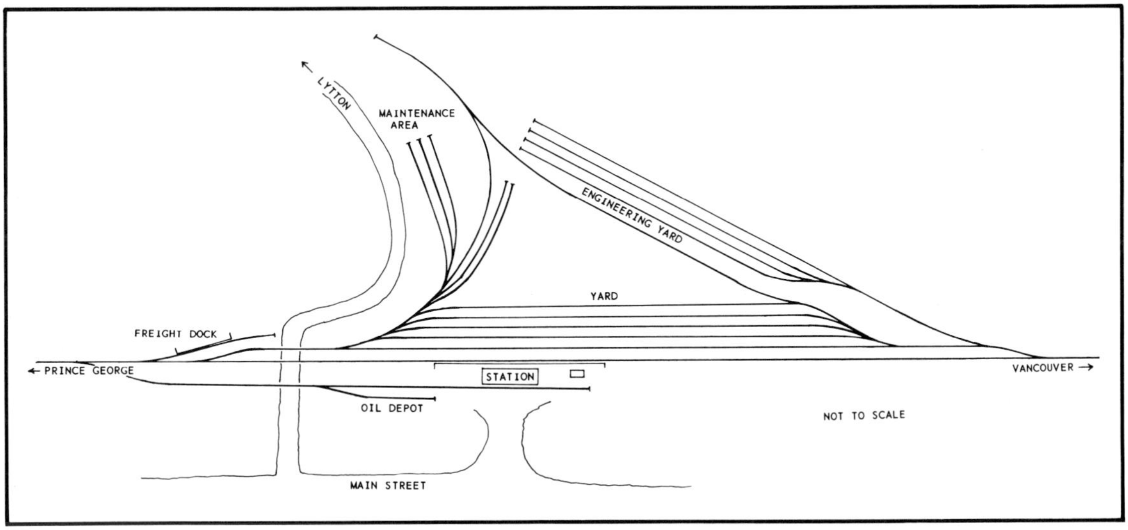

CLEARANCE
NOT
STANDARD
STOP
DERAIL

woodchips, lime, sulphur and even jade. Southbound trains carry these products to Vancouver for distribution and are given superiority over most northbound traffic on the single line. Northbound trains are often formed mainly of empty stock, although there is also considerable traffic in construction materials for projects in the remote north country. The railway also carries substantial 'piggyback' traffic in road trailers destined for points in the north and on to the Alaska highway.

**Left: Lillooet station looking north in September 1981. The small building is an office. Note the flagpole and the passenger assistance steps.**

**Below left: General view looking south from the level crossing. The RDC is stabled in the siding, and on its right the oil depot siding is protected by a derail clipped to the rail-head (catch points are not provided). The smoke is caused by burning 'slash', the debris left after logging operations.**

**Below: The 'Indian train' formed of BCR Alco No 560 and coach BCOL 8 wittily named *Budd Wiser*. In the background, fuel tank wagons and cabooses are stabled.**

The freight is moved in long trains, often with up to eight locomotives, three or four of which are placed in mid-train position and operated by radio control from the cab of the leading locomotive. Several special types of freight car are used for forest products, including high-sided 70-ton gondolas for woodchips, bulkhead flatcars for wrapped boards and high-stake cars for logs. Most other vehicles are standard types of box cars, gondolas, hoppers and flatcars similar to those used in the USA. Indeed freightcars from South of the border are often to be seen on the BCR while those of Canada's other major railways are in regular use. Private-owner cars, particularly those of the lumber industry, add a splash of colour among the green of BCR vehicles. Among those to be seen around Lillooet are the blue of Mountain Pine Lumber, and the red and white of Canadian Forest Products (Canfor).

Passenger traffic on the BCR is sparse by comparison, but Lillooet is probably one of the best places to see the line's passenger services. There is a daily service to Lillooet from North Vancouver, worked by Budd diesel railcars (RDCs). Lillooet is reached at 12.35 and on

Mondays, Thursdays and Saturdays, the train divides there and the main portion continues to Prince George, 300 miles further north. Depending on the formation, one or two cars are left at Lillooet to return to North Vancouver, departing at 15.25. On Tuesdays, Fridays and Sundays there is a southbound journey from Prince George to Lillooet where the morning arrival from Vancouver joins it to return south as one train. On Wednesdays there is no service north of Lillooet in either direction.

The daily North Vancouver-Lillooet service is

**Above left: The maintenance area, looking towards the main line. In the centre is the wheel change gantry and on the right, one of several office cabins.**

**Left: A southbound freight with 'trailer on flatcar' (TOFC) traffic much in evidence.** *J. G. Greenall*

**Above: The level crossing with the wrappers still on the warning lights. Beyond the disused freight dock are further BCR buildings.**

supplemented by an unadvertised morning train between Seton Portage and Lillooet. The empty stock leaves Lillooet at 05.45 and returns from Seton Portage at 07.15, arriving Lillooet at 08.10. This curious train is described in the working timetable as a mixed train, but is in fact a school special which collects Indian children from the villages of Seton, Shalalth, Retaskit and Macneil and brings them in to school at Lillooet. They return home on the normal afternoon service. The morning special is a remarkable formation consisting of an elderly 1,600hp diesel locomotive and a solitary passenger car (on six-wheel bogies) complete with a wood-burning stove and tall chimney.

Extra traffic to and from Lillooet yard is generated by the presence of the engineer's yard there, while several of the longer loops provide storage for surplus rolling stock not immediately required for traffic. In recent years Lillooet has even seen the occasional steam working. The provincial government sponsors the operation of ex-CPR 'Royal Hudson' 4-6-4 No 2860 between North Vancouver and Squamish, and also owns a travelling museum exhibition train which is usually headed by ex-CPR 2-8-0 No 3716. Although the 'Royal Hudson' does not normally work as far as Lillooet, one could stretch a point for modelling purposes. Certainly it has worked through to Pemberton for a special occasion, while No 3716 must have passed through Lillooet several times on its extensive tours with the provincial Museum Train.

**Modelling possibilities**

Even a small (by Canadian standards) station like Lillooet will take up a vast space when modelled in HO scale, so considerable compression is necessary. However, provided care is taken to preserve the essential features and particularly the 'apparent' spaciousness of the location, a satisfactory model is possible. My 19ft long loft leaves some 14ft for the station area, allowing 3ft radius curves at the ends. The baseboard is a nominal 2ft wide, with a projection at the front to

Above: The sand store shed and adjacent loading tower.

Above right: Lillooet's 1921-built station. The waiting room is at the nearer end, while the bay window below the nameboard houses the despatcher's office. Note the air-conditioner attached to the upper front wall.

accommodate the main features of the 'wye'. The curve to the 'south' of the station will skirt the shore of Seton Lake, with the scenery becoming more rugged through a canyon section around the end of the loft. There will then be provision for some hidden sidings behind the scenery on the other long side of the layout. This will feature a typical flag stop (halt) and a high trestle bridge where the scenery becomes very narrow alongside the trap door.

The curve to the north of the station will feature an industrial facility — probably a pulp mill or a 'chipper' — served by a private siding with its own shunter. The station area also features a small industrial facility in the form of an oil distribution terminal. This is an ideal small modelling project which consists of a small yard with tanks, office and loading facilities for road tankers, The oil, probably domestic heating fuel and petrol for distribution to outlying communities, is brought in by rail and off-loaded through a solitary gantry to the storage tanks.

The various structures in the rail yard could also be tackled as small individual modelling projects. The 'Indian special' is stabled here during the day, its locomotive being available for any shunting work which might be required. In addition, it would not be unusual to find a locomotive coming or going with engineer's equipment. The RDC forming the morning train from Vancouver lays over in the siding behind the station building until shortly before the arrival of the section from Prince George. It then moves up to the turnout, awaits the arrival of the southbound train and follows it into the station to couple up. The railcars are fuelled at the station

platform using a hose drawn from a manhole between the tracks.

Although no freight trains are actually timetabled to cross at Lillooet, late running or the operation of 'extras' could well mean that this would happen. Extras are trains not included in the timetabled paths and can result from special operating requirements, such as the need to run a train in more than one section. Motive power consists of a variety of diesels from 1,600hp to 3,000hp and BCR has a current fleet of around 120, some of them little more than a year old. Most of the early lower powered types are Alcos, while later 2,000-3,000hp types were built by their Canadian successors, Montreal Locomotive Works. The most recent additions are the ubiquitous General Motors SD 40-2s, of which BCR has twelve.

There are no really accurate models of BCR's Alcos readily available as proprietary models, but there are a number which can easily be converted or super-detailed. Mehanotehnika produces the 1,600hp Alco RS3 in the guise of a bright green SNCF locomotive in one of its inexpensive European train sets. The 1,800hp RS11 is available from Model Power in BCR livery, but needs a little work and a good repaint. Tyco's Alco Century 420 is not too far from the 2,500hp Alcos in the BCR fleet, and apart from the bogie wheelbase, the AHM Alco Century 628 will pass for the BCR's MLW 630 3,000hp units. AHM have produced an SD 40, but to be really accurate the longer SD40-2 as used by BCR is available from GSB Rail. Much of the readily available freight stock can be used, although for those modelling the current scene, bulkhead flats and really big chip cars are notably absent from the proprietary ranges. On the passenger stock side, the Athearn RDC is ideal, especially if re-powered with one of the little Tenshodo 'spud' motor bogies, but it is produced in batches and sometimes difficult to obtain.

Modelling a prototype location which is 4,500 miles distant presents its problems but it is a real challenge and certainly no one can accuse it of being just 'another GWR branch line!'

# 'Thunder's Hill'

## A 3mm Layout by *Peter Bossom*

*This 3mm Scale layout was exhibited at the Model Railway Club's 1982 exhibition*

The origin of this layout goes back to a portable model built at short notice to fill a space in my local club's first exhibition in the early '70s. The original and its 'New and Improved' successor gave much enjoyment, but both suffered from being long and thin which meant taking over most of the house for an operating session. Whilst this was tolerated, it was not particularly satisfactory and thought was given to a layout which would fit my shed — or any *one* room, look authentic, give as much enjoyment as past layouts and still be portable. The shed allowed a maximum size of 9ft by 5ft and most cars seem capable of taking boards 3ft 6in long, with comfort. After some deliberation an overall size of 7ft by 5ft was settled upon. The board width of 1ft 2in gives just enough room for two operators inside the well, if required, and keeps the weight to reasonable limits for transportation. Like many

**Below: Thunders Hill station, with 0-6-2T No 2505 departing on a local service.**

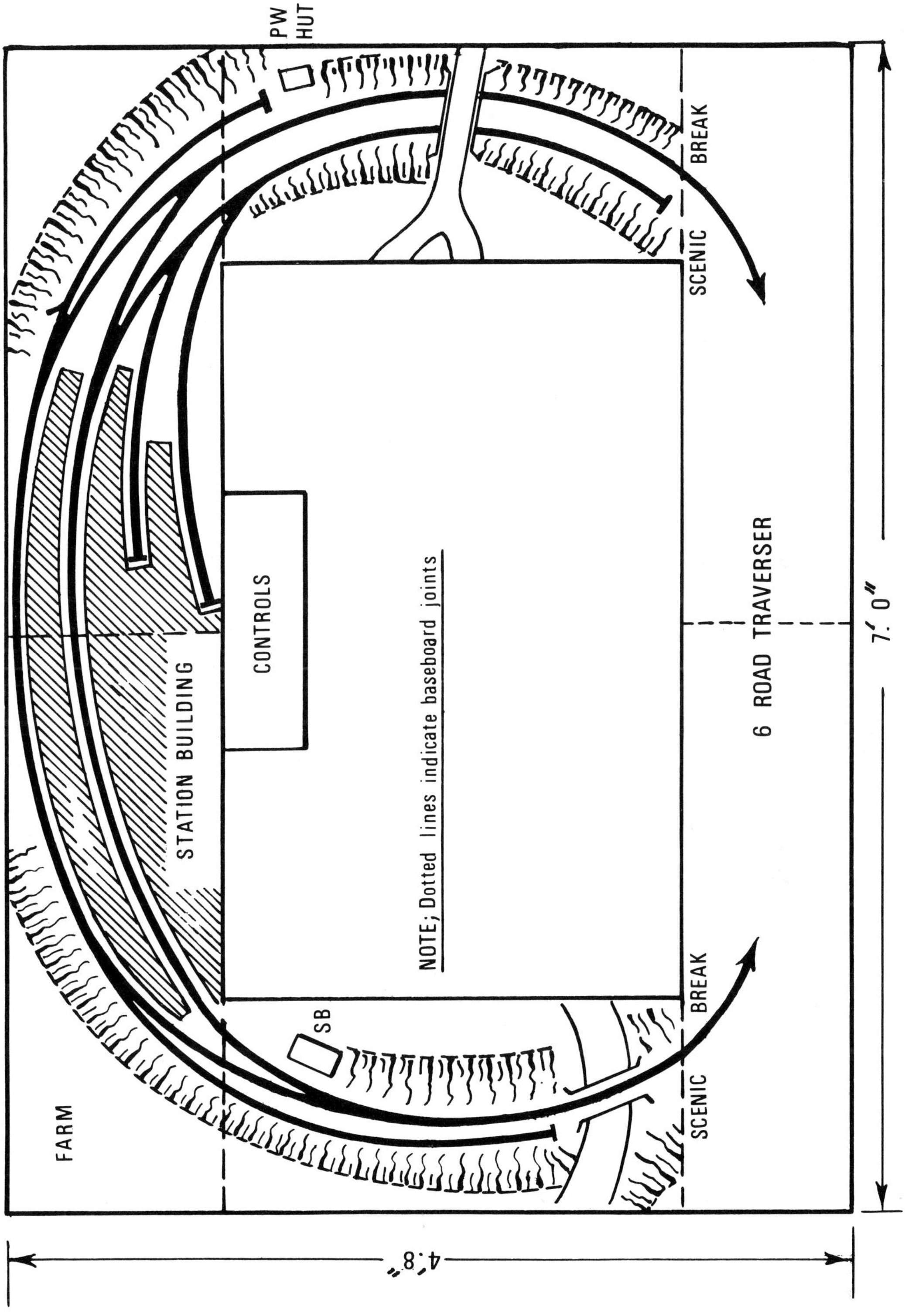
PW HUT
BREAK
SCENIC
STATION BUILDING
CONTROLS
NOTE; Dotted lines indicate baseboard joints
6 ROAD TRAVERSER
7' 0"
SB
BREAK
SCENIC
FARM
4' 8"

modellers I bolt two boards face to face for transporting — and the bigger the boards etc etc. I model the Central Section, Southern Railway, ex-LBSCR territory, and my modelling tends to be representative rather than specific. Within these guidelines I finally chose to use the track plan of Hellingly Station on the Cuckoo line as a basis for my model, but with the setting on the ill-fated LBSCR Ouse Valley project. The prototype layout was followed fairly closely, with the island platform incorporated, but the tramway branch to the nearby mental hospital removed. This had no real effect on operating potential and created a relatively unusual station layout in the process. A map published in the *Railway Magazine* indicated the approximate route of the Ouse Valley line and in consultation with an Ordnance Survey map, it was decided that the line might

**Above left and left: SR 0-6-2T No 2480 with a 'Birdcage' set, seen working outward and return journeys under the road bridge .**

**Above: Exterior view of Thunders Hill station showing how well the style of a typical LBSCR station has been captured.**

have passed through, or near to Thunders Hill on its way from Uckfield to Hellingly. (Thunders Hill does exist, along with Pick Hill, Gun Hill and Muddles Green, all in the same area!)

I now had all the ingredients and the next step was to bind them together! The track plan was sketched out full size to see how — and if — it fitted the boards, which by some miracle it did quite well. This sketch was then turned into a working diagram and tracklaying commenced. My previous layout had been my first attempt at soldered trackwork and it had worked quite well, despite each point being made as a separate unit. This time I decided to build the trackwork in as big a unit as possible. Fine in theory although a bit fraught in practice, with yard lengths of rail swinging about as you squint at bits and pieces! Despite the dangers I finally ended up with the required formations tested, painted, laid and ballasted. Since a string of wagons propelled by hand exhibit different characteristics to the same string propelled over the same section of track by a locomotive something had to be done about the electrics.

I had previously conducted my own survey among exhibitors seeking the best controller available (not an easy task as everybody had their own favourite!) and finally decided upon an ECM Compspeed. This decision has not been regretted as it does wonders for my old Tri-ang 3-pole motors. This was duly inserted into the control panel along with a multitude of switches. It all looks very complicated, but it isn't. I'm a simple soul and the electrics on all my layouts are a reflection of the installer! The switches, 9 in all and a 12-way rotary are section switches, enabling me to hold a loco more or less wherever I choose, although only two are in constant use. All points are operated by H&M solenoids through a CDU and old Hornby-Dublo switches.

Scenery is the part I really enjoy, it's messy, it's quick — especially if you use plaster of Paris bandages as for holding broken limbs, (my local chemist is still wondering what I wanted them for!) and you can let your imagination run (gentle) riot. Being a small layout it was possible to give some attention to detail and I have tried to create a number of small scenes within the model. These include a flock of sheep being moved from one field to another, a group of three men unloading a railway wagon — well, one is unloading and two are chatting. The farm is cluttered with a mixture of bits and pieces interspersed with chickens scratching about everywhere and a herd of cows, plodding through the yard. The few passengers on the station platform have been

SOUTHERN
2480

SOUTHERN
1902

**Left: No 2480 passing a typical SR platelayer's hut.**

**Bottom left: There's plenty of atmosphere in this view of SR 2-6-0 No 1902 leaving Thunders Hill as the local bus passes under the line.**

**Below and bottom: The Thunders Hill layout, set up ready for an open air operating session.**

altered to make them more life-like, and to complete the scene a few birds have been added. Following the persuasive writings of Alan Downes, the buildings have been individually tiled where necessary. Once or twice I did wonder just what I had taken on but the finished effect is worth the effort!

Signalling is very simple, up and down starters are provided, together with a number of ground signals in the correct places. To add interest the

**Above: Thunders Hill signalbox is a Saxby & Farmer structure, typical of LBSCR practice.**

up starter is a short rail-built SR upper quadrant signal, whereas the down starter is the original ex-LBSCR lower quadrant type. Due to sighting problems with the existing signals, banner repeaters have been installed at the opposite ends of each platform. Both starters are operated by H&M solenoids — if only because I can never actually find any of the ex GPO solenoids that so many modellers write about!

The goods vehicle fleet could be described as ample, totalling some 60 vehicles. Coaching stock is limited to a 4-car 'Balloon' set, a 3-car 'birdcage', two Maunsell restriction 'O' coaches and a single 'balloon' auto-trailer. They just cover the passenger services, but leave no spares. There are sufficient locomotives to cover the trains run, with a couple left over just in case, but the mixture is not quite right. Perhaps one day . . . ! Most of the stock is scratch-built on various proprietary chassis, although where possible use has been made of Tri-ang products and the excellent kits marketed by the Three Millimetre Society. I use liveries appropriate to 1937, which to my mind indicated a mixture of old (awaiting painting) and new (just painted) styles.

Operation is by sequence covering a day's working. The original sequence compiled using a 'Cuckoo Line' Working Timetable had some 54 moves. Pruning produced a workable sequence of 24 moves and the whole thing takes about an hour to run through. This puts most of the stock back where it started and within 5 min the rest is replaced and we start again. Thought has been given to a train indicator but without much success at present — and since over-confident operators have been known to miss out complete trains perhaps it is better not to have a public timetable!

This then is Thunders Hill, a bit of fact and a bit of fiction. My thanks must go to many who have helped — in particular my family for putting up with everything, Martin for his photos, 'Arch' for his troubleshooting and John who travels incredible distances just to operate!. Many other have unwittingly assisted by displaying their work at exhibitions and in the model press, where other people's ideas have been — and are — freely and unashamedly poached!

# Picture parade

**Left: Head-on view of Lynton & Barnstaple Railway 2-6-2T *Yeo* at Pilton in 1935.** *A. B. McLeod*

**Below: Otterington station was rebuilt in 1933 to accommodate quadrupling of the main line between York-Northallerton. The structures, seen here just after completion, make a perfect contemporary setting for 'A4' Pacifics.**

**Left: Original cab-end design of Derby Lightweight dmu. Note mu jumper connections.** *BR*

**Below: Midland Railway lattice footbridge at Evesham.**

**Right: SR Bulleid 'Q1' 0-6-0 No 33019.** *D. Sutton/Ian Allan Library*

**Far right: The latest in station nameboards, and an elderly platform trolley.** *M. Soden*

**Below right: Swindon Cross-country dmu fitted with headlight for Central Wales line service.** *A. Swain*

**Below far right: Upper quadrant signal at New Holland in 1980.** *P. Harris*

33019

Ardlui

# An automatic turntable

## *Robert Fysh* EM Gauge Society

A turntable is always a focal point on any layout. Whilst operating other people's layouts I have found that it is all too easy to forget a locomotive which is being turned, especially if the turntable is being rotated at scale speed. One gets totally involved in accepting or despatching a train or doing some shunting and the next time you look at the turntable the locomotive is facing the same way, having done a complete rotation!

The solution is an automatic turntable as shown in the accompanying diagrams. The idea is to have a disc of steel or plywood mounted rigidly on the turntable spindle, so as to turn with it. The disc has two cut-outs so that the roller on the arm of the microswitch drops into one thus breaking the current to the turntable motor, when the tracks are in alignment.

The microswitches I use are the miniature type made by Burgess, catalogue number VCFYR 1 or VCSP2YR1 and can be obtained cheaply from radio/electrical surplus stores. A push button is incorporated in the circuit to by-pass the microswitch and start the turntable rotating. It is best to lay the tracks up to the turntable last so that the correct alignment can be guaranteed. Of course, if you require more than two tracks from the turntable further cut outs in the disc can be made.

**Below: Outriggers are used to get a quart into a pint pot as No 7808 *Cookham Manor* is turned at Ludgershall on 10 September 1961.** *R. E. James-Robertson*

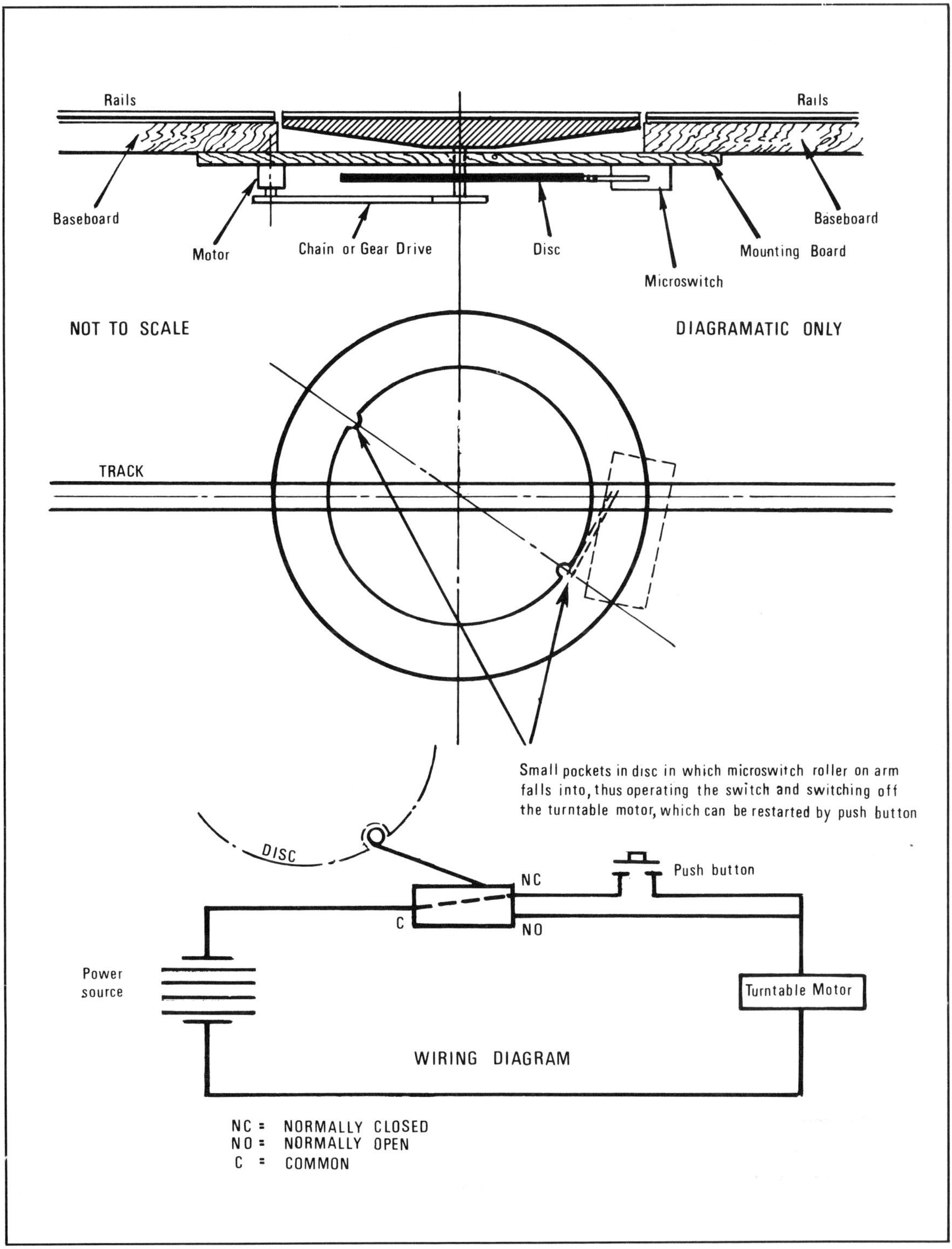
Rails
Rails
Baseboard
Motor
Chain or Gear Drive
Disc
Microswitch
Mounting Board
Baseboard
NOT TO SCALE
DIAGRAMATIC ONLY
TRACK
Small pockets in disc in which microswitch roller on arm falls into, thus operating the switch and switching off the turntable motor, which can be restarted by push button
DISC
NC
Push button
C
NO
Power source
Turntable Motor
WIRING DIAGRAM
NC = NORMALLY CLOSED
NO = NORMALLY OPEN
C = COMMON

# A really simple points detection circuit

*C. P. Boocock*

Modellers with large layouts, or with hidden loops, sidings or junctions, often have points or even double slips that cannot be seen from the operating position. If points are wrongly set, the resultant derailment can be difficult to rectify if it occurs in an inaccessible location. How is the operator to be sure that points have changed to the correct direction and that all routes are properly set?

A useful aid would be small detection lights on the control panel that would indicate the actual point setting. For example in Fig 1, when the points are set for route A the control panel indicator on the exit from the points for route A is lit, while that on route B is not. When the points are changed to route B the route A light goes out and the route B light comes on. Thus the operator can tell at a glance if the route setting is correct.

The circuit necessary to achieve this is very simple indeed, particularly if the popular H&M SM3 point motor is used. Only four, cheap electronic components are needed. These are two miniature 2mm diameter, light emitting diodes (LEDs) which can be red, yellow or green, one ordinary diode capable of withstanding 20 volts, and one $\frac{1}{4}$ Watt resistor of around 500 ohms. The circuit is shown in diagram form in Fig 2. It uses the 16V ac separate supply available from the side sockets on most H&M controller/ transformers

To produce the circuit described, a wire is run from one 16V ac socket to the underside of the control panel and the small 500 ohm resistor soldered on. Two wires are led from this, each being soldered to the input (the longer) leg of either of the LEDs in the control panel. From the shorter (output) legs one wire is run to each of the switch terminals numbered 4 and 5 on the SM3 point motor. From the point motor terminal 3 a single return wire is run to the second 16V ac terminal on the controller. A single diode should be inserted in this return wire with the end of the diode that is marked with a white collar set towards the controller terminal. This diode is to prevent interference by any currents circulating from other circuits that may by linked to the same terminal sockets.

We have a particularly troublesome spot on our Weybourne layout where any rear-end collisions are extremely difficult to rerail and hold up operations for minutes on end. The offending hidden points now have this circuit fitted. The operator has no excuse now, and all he has to do is to keep his eye on the control board.

One other valuable feature of this detection circuit is that if for any reason the point motor fails to throw, the fact is clearly evident. The lights on the panel do not change over.

Peco point motors have no built-in auxiliary switch and it is therefore necessary to make one's own in order to apply point detection.

FIG.1 PART OF CONTROL PANEL

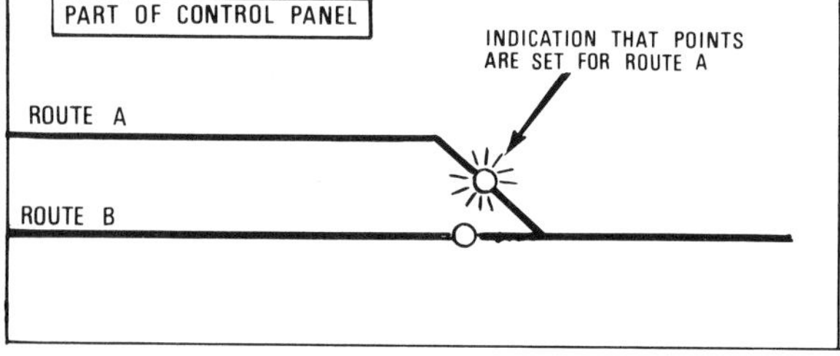


FIG.2 POINT DETECTION CIRCUIT

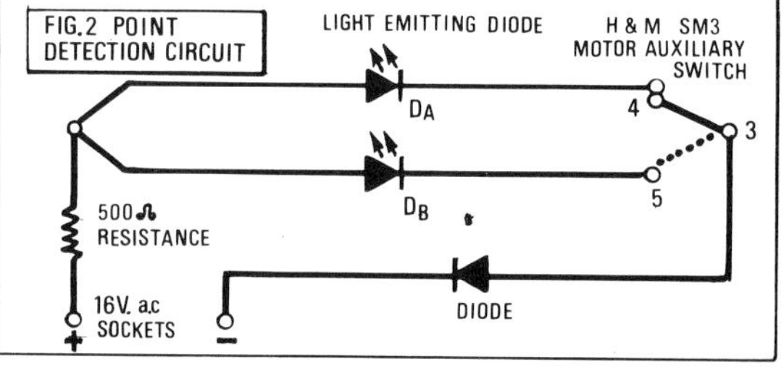

Datafile 3

# BR Class 03 0-6-0 shunter

Since the motive power rationalisation of the late 1960s, the Class 03 shunter has been the standard small 204hp diesel shunter design. The Class is, however, confined to the Eastern and Western Regions, the LMR and SR using the larger 350hp types and the Scottish Region using the small Class 06 0-4-0s as well as the Class 08s. Some 230 Class 03s were built by BR and originally numbered D2000-199 and D2370-D2399. Externally, they were similar in outline to the Drewry-built Class 04s, prototype of the Airfix diesel shunter kit which is now out of production.

The BR diagram of a standard vacuum braked 03 is reproduced here to show the main dimensions, but since their introduction in 1957 the locomotives have been subject to modification and several variants now exist. The most major alterations have resulted from the fitting of dual air and vacuum brakes, or from the adaptation of some locomotives to the reduced height loading gauge of the ex-Bury Port and Gwendraeth Valley line in South Wales. Locomotives fitted

**Below: Class 03 0-6-0 No D2002 in original green livery.**
*F. W. Day*

with air brakes have an air tank mounted vertically in front of the cab on the left side, and carry additional buffer beam pipes. Some examples also have air pipe connections mounted at 'waist' level to suit operation with mu or coaching stock.

Locomotives Nos 03.119/30/41/2/4/5/51/2 and 03.382 have had their cab height reduced by 4½in to suit the reduced height of engineering works on the BPGV line. These locomotives usually work in trios to cope with the severe gradients on this line. Other differences between members of the class are mainly matters of detail, and anyone modelling a Class 03 locomotive would do well to work from photographs of a particular example. Single or dual horns can be fitted, and some 03s have the tapered exhaust 'chimney' similar to that fitted to Drewry locomotives. At one time, 03s used in Weymouth carried a bell, which is a statutory requirement for working over the street tramway to Weymouth Quay.

Some ER-based examples work with a match wagon. This is not the old GWR-style shunter's 'runner', but appears to be a former 4-wheel Conflat wagon. The match wagons are used because the 03 can sometimes fail to activate track circuits when running light, and the addition

**Below: Later livery and alternative exhaust stack on No D2167.** *R. C. Riley*

**Bottom: No D2196, air-braked and fitted with high-level jumper cables.** *J. Scrace*

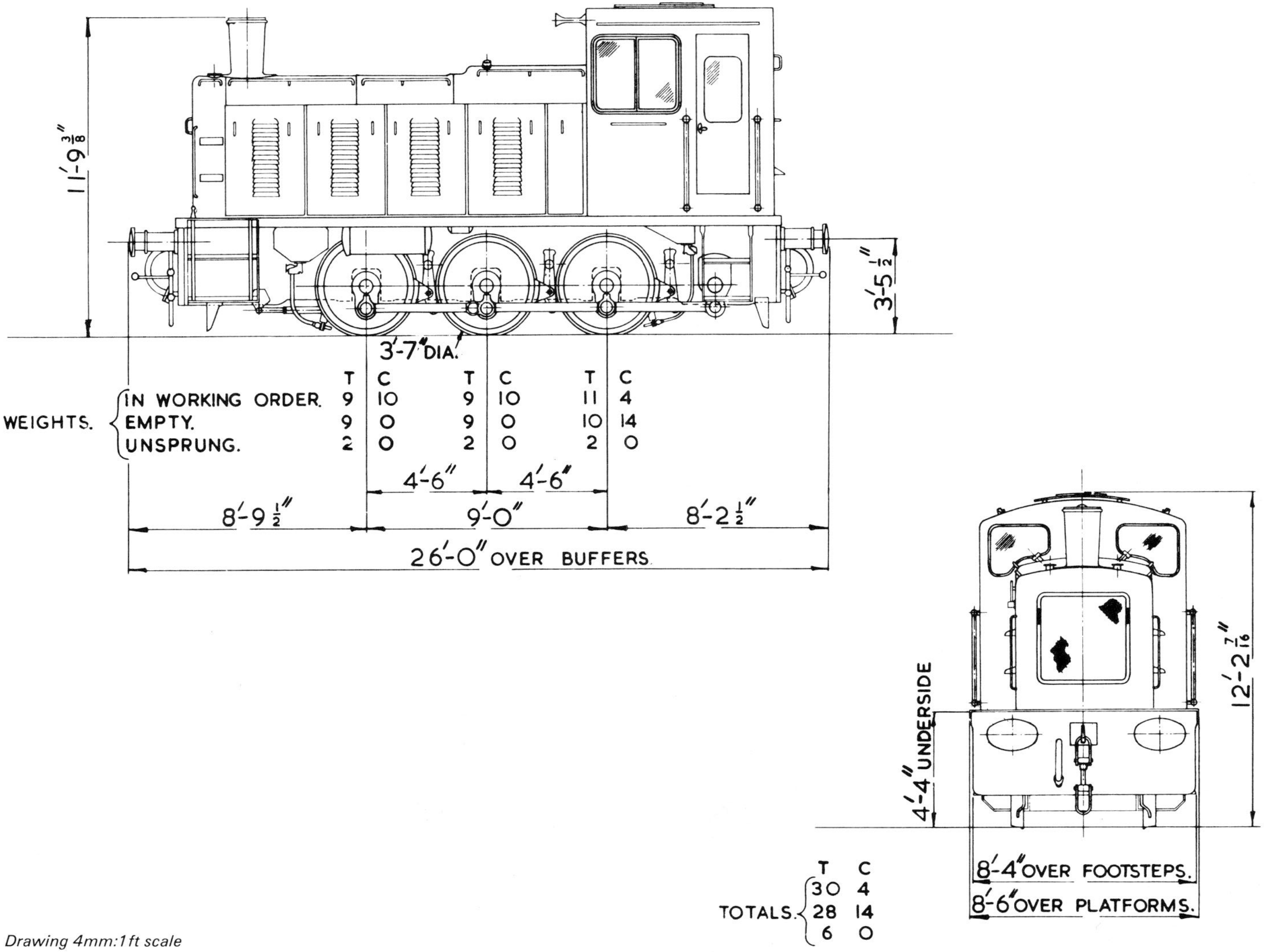


Drawing 4mm:1ft scale

**Top: One of the Weymouth Quay 03s with air brakes and additional toolboxes, bell and flashing light.** *J. Scrace*

**Above: An 03 in current livery, No 03.196 is air-braked.** *B. J. Nicolle*

of one vehicle alleviates this problem. The present livery of the class is BR blue with black and yellow chevrons on front and back to make them conspicuous. Buffer beams are yellow, and the BR logo, number and information panel are carried in white on the cabsides. The original livery was BR green with red buffer beams, some of the earlier examples being delivered without the black and yellow chevrons. Coupling rods were originally in natural metallic finish, but nowadays may also be in either white or yellow.

Although usually confined to station pilot and light shunting work, the 03s have found extensive use on freight branches and sidings, and in docks areas. In their early years they were even found on the occasional passenger working, the workmen's trains on the Swindon-Highworth branch being a case in point. More recently, in addition to working the BPGV line, members of the class have been used for trip-workings on the Central Wales line, where they are now the only locomotives permitted. In recent years withdrawals have steadily reduced the numbers of 03s in traffic, and with steadily reducing requirements for shunters it seem unlikely that the class will survive much beyond the next couple of years.

# Small Structures 3

# Savernake water tank

This interesting little building formed the water tank at Savernake High Level station on the Midland and South Western Junction Railway. The M&SWJR line was closed in 1961, and the High Level station closed two or three years earlier, when Cheltenham-Andover services were diverted over the Marlborough branch and into the ex-GWR Low Level station. However, this water tank and the adjacent signalbox have survived in a derelict state in the grounds of a bungalow-conversion of the station building.

The brick structure housed a hot-air engine which was used to pump water up to the tank. It was constructed of red and grey engineers' bricks, with a grey slate roof. The tank, still painted in GWR light and dark stone, was supplied by Stothert & Pitt, and carried an oval maker's plate on the front. A ladder from the station platform gave access to the inspection hatch, and there

**Below: The disused water tank and pump house at Savernake High Level.**

Drawing 4mm — 1ft scale

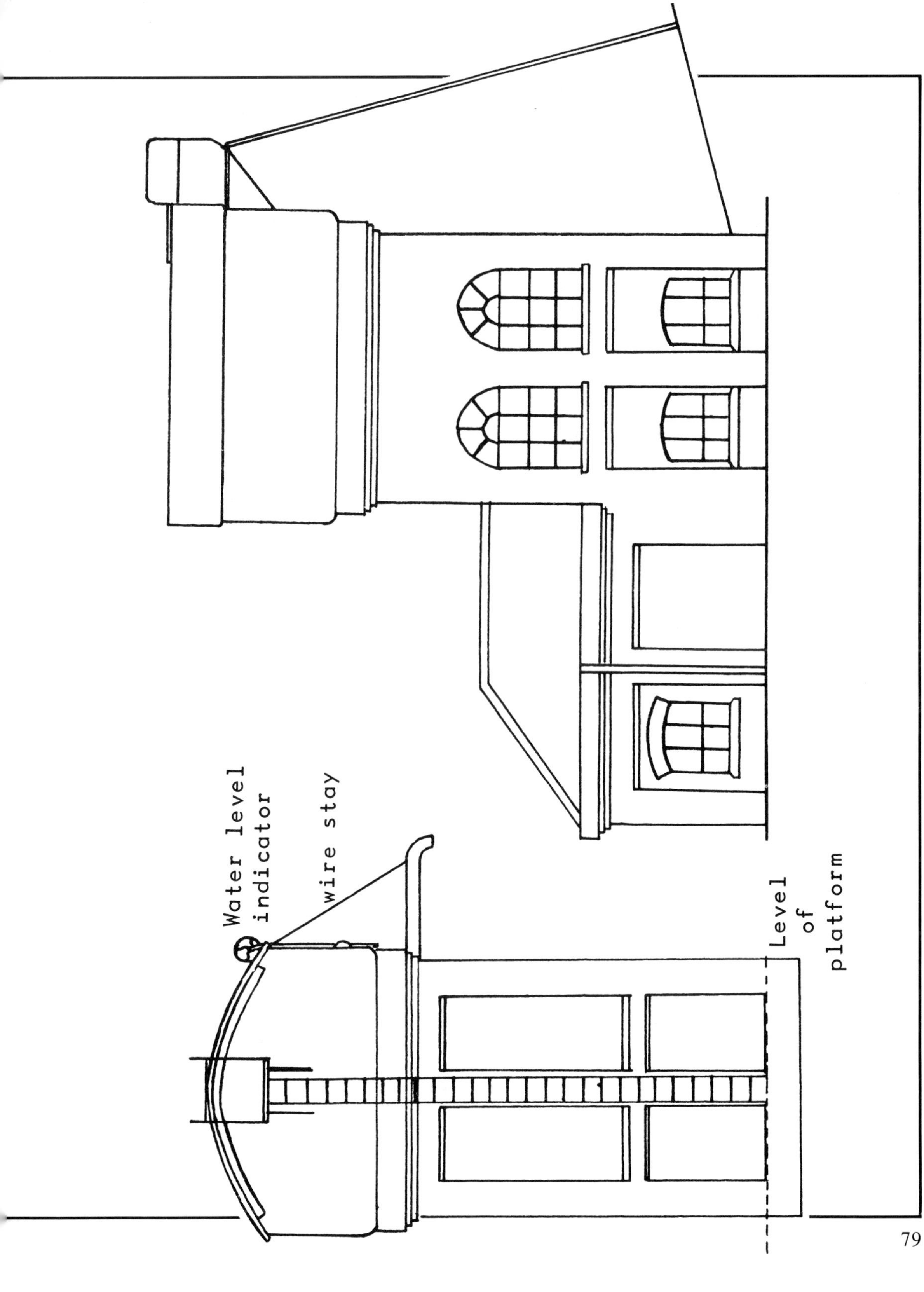
Water level indicator
wire stay
Level of platform

**Above and left: Two more views of the disused water tank and pumphouse.**

was a crude water-level indicator, consisting of a pointer on a piece of chain, running over a pulley and connected to a float in the tank. Thus when the tank was full, the pointer would be at its lowest!

The main outflow pipe would originally have had a 'bag' and possibly some further pipework incorporating a flexible joint, but all trace of this, and the operating valve arrangement, have disappeared. Important points for the modeller to note are the details of the brickwork, with recesses and arched windows, and the very slim glazing bars which add character to the structure.

# Canfor's SW 1200RS

Canadian Forest Products Limited (Canfor) owns and operates North America's longest main line logging railway, the 75 miles from Vernon via Woss Lake to Beaver Cove on Vancouver Island, British Columbia. The railway follows the valley of the Nimpkish River, starting some 20 miles north of Gold River in the remote and beautiful north of the island. Its story, and the history of the various companies which now constitute Canfor, is well told in Robert Turner's excellent book *Vancouver Island Railroads*.

After years of steam operation which included a large collection of Pacific Coast Shays, and eventually the last working steamer in Canadian Logging (a 2-8-0), Canfor is an all-diesel road using EMD SW1200RS road switchers. The SW 1200RS is a main line version, or 'Sport model' of the standard SW 1200 switcher and is only to be found in Canada. It includes a high capacity fuel tank and dynamic braking. These features result in very obvious external changes, as the large fuel tank displaces the air tanks from the underframe to a position atop the hood immediately ahead of the dynamic brake radiator housing. In addition, Canfor's locomotives have the Flexicoil trucks obtainable as an option on the SW 1200, but they do not have the modified number boards and fairings normally associated with Canadian SW 1200s.

**Below: The unpainted model, with added details shown in white.**

I felt that a model of one of the Canfor road switchers in its striking yellow paint and with the extra fittings, would add some variety amid my green British Columbia Railway stock, and would also provide a useful industrial switcher for all those Life-Like Thrall boxcars in Canfor colours. One problem faces those of us who model North American equipment many miles away in the UK, and that is the difficulty in obtaining prototype data and small modelling parts. I offer this as my excuse if I have made any obvious mistakes or if I seem to have gone the long way round to do some simple job.

I began with the Athearn SW 1500 model, and I should perhaps point out at this stage that I wanted to make a reasonable representation of the prototype. I was not, however, setting out to achieve rivet-counting accuracy. Some of the small louvres on the Athearn hood are incorrectly placed for the SW 1200, but otherwise it seems to fulfil requirements. The first job is to separate the body from the chassis by prising off the lugs behind the fuel tank mouldings. The cab and headlight glazing pieces were then removed and the cab and hood mouldings separated.

At this stage, the hood was cut as shown in the diagram and the headlight mouldings were trimmed off with a sharp knife and filed flat. I also removed the various moulded-on steps and drilled holes ready to replace these with wire. The air tank detail and associated pipework was carved off the faces of the fuel tank using a razor saw and the surfaces were then smoothed up with a file. This concluded the cutting work.

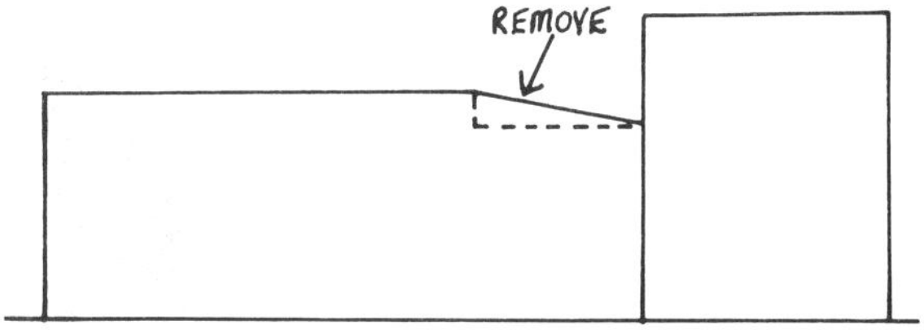


Most of the small parts needed are available from Detail Associates. I used the following:

Mars dual headlight EMD switcher type with number boards
Nathan MP5 air horns (AH 1602)
Lift rings EMD switcher type
Cab sunshades (SS1301)
EMD type drop steps (early) (DS 1401)
Radio Antenna, Sinclair type (RA 1803)

In addition, Flexicoil truck sideframes are available from Juneco, leaving only the dynamic brake unit and the air tanks to be manufactured. I was unable to trace a source of either of these items, although the dynamic brake fan is now available in North America.

I used 30 thou styrene sheet for the dynamic brake housing and began by filling the cut area of the hood with two pieces, one shaped to fit vertically inside the hood and the other to provide the flat base for the housing. The circular fan grille was cut from the top of a scrapped Tyco F-unit body and the housing was then built up from styrene sheet around this. The sides of the housing measure 15mm by 10mm high and the front and back 18mm by 10mm high. The side louvres were scored on the styrene using a sharp scriber and when the solvent adhesive had dried all joins were filled with automobile filler and filed smooth. The unit is cemented in place against the vertical front of the recess leaving a gap between the rear of the housing and the cab.

Two pieces of 5mm dia brass tube 35mm long formed the air tanks. Pieces of brass rod were

soldered into the ends of each piece and the domed ends were formed by a little careful turning in the chuck of a power tool. The saddles on which the tanks are carried were cut to shape from styrene sheet and fixed to the hood with solvent adhesive. The ends of the tanks were first drilled to receive the pipework, and cemented in place with suitable impact adhesive. Pipework was added from soft wire. I then fitted the various detail items, headlights, radio antenna, and lift rings as shown in white in the accompanying photograph. To prevent risk of damage, the horns, sunshades and drop steps were not fitted until immediately before painting.

Next I added the various steps and handrails on the hood using soft wire, together with the two small hand rails on the cab rear. The ditch lights are castings from a short/lived detail kit which I attempted unsuccessfully to market in North America. Similar items may be available, but if not they can be simply turned up in the chuck of an electric drill. At this stage the cab and hood were reassembled, omitting the cab glazing until after painting. The remaining jobs included filling in the area between the drop step and the rear platform to form an extra step, using pieces of styrene sheet, and fitting Athearn handrails. The enlarged fuel tanks were formed of several layers of styrene laminated to the desired thickness and then shamfered with a file to the correct shape. These were then fixed in place over the remains of the moulded tank.

The radio antenna, sunshades and horns were installed next. The horns consist of about eleven tiny mouldings and require great care and patience in assembly. I reinforced the stem of the completed unit with a tiny piece of wire to make it slightly more resistant to damage.

The completed body was given several coats of matt yellow applied with an air brush. On reflection it might have been wise to spray the black plastic moulding with a matt grey or white first as it proved difficult to cover satisfactorily with the yellow. I used *Rail Canada Volume 2* as a guide to the colour scheme. However, the three locomotives on the Canfor roster (Nos 301-3) do seem to show some detail differences. Not all of them appear to have ditch lights, and some illustrations show them with the wording Canadian Forest Products Limited in full. Others show just Canadian Forest Products, and recent view, suggests that the wording on the hood has been abandoned in favour of just a Canfor logo on the cab side.

In addition, one of the illustrations in *Rail Canada* appears to show No 303 as having the truck sideframes painted in a pale colour — certainly not black. In fact it would appear to be yellow as used on the bodywork, and I adopted this style for my model.

Various black lining materials are available, including self adhesive tapes, dry transfers and decals. I used waterslide decals as I find these easier to position accurately. The Canadian Forest Products lettering was applied with Letraset on to a piece of clear decal material. This was then applied to the model as a normal decal, but if a decal setting solution is used this must be kept well away from the Letraset or it will dissolve the lettering. Striping on the pilots was from a Microscale Canadian Pacific decal sheet. For the time being the models retains it original Athearn truck sideframes.

**Below left and below: Two views of the completed SW-1200RS model.**

# Overspill

## - Scenario for a layout

*T. W. Kirtley*

This layout has been designed to satisfy a set of clearly defined requirements.

There is, of course, nothing unusual in that. Most layouts are basically a result of their designer having worked through a series of realistic criteria, satisfying as many as possible, and sensibly compromising on the remainder. What I think may be of interest to other modellers is that in this case some of the requirements and constraints appeared incompatible, but eventually all were satisfied.

The layout requirements were as follows:

(1) The layout must be a means by which I could run, and watch, any type of train which could be seen in the north-east of England, ranging from express passenger and trunk freight to push-pull passenger. I have always been an inveterate train watcher and a model railway, to me, is principally a means of recreating such lost scenes. However, I can think of nothing more boring than watching stereotyped branch-liners wearing the tracks away when I could be watching the multifarious steam-hauled trains of the North Eastern Railway and its successors. This obviously required a layout with a large running stock and a variety of train formations, and therefore tending towards the larger main line scene.

(2) Notwithstanding requirement 1, the layout must be capable of authentic operation with sustained interest and not be a replica of the 1925 S&D procession.

(3) The layout should incorporate a number of favorite lineside and architectural features and have an authentic atmosphere.

(4) In spite of the inherent complexity inevitable from requirements 1, 2 and 3, the layout should be capable of single-handed or multi-operator working.

(5) Capital expenditure must be the minimum consistent with 1-4 above.

(6) This is where the difficulty arises, since all this must be done in a space of 8ft 7in by 7ft 4in, that being the size of the spare third bedroom in our 'modern' semi.

A short consideration of points 1, 2 and 3 eliminated branch lines and led to the general conclusion that the layout must reflect NER practice in a north eastern city. However, in most large cities served by the NER, for example York, Newcastle and Leeds, the principal station would be a through station, and even in model form this requires a vast stock to maintain the endless procession of trains without resorting to too much repetition. Capable as A4's were, they did not perform many London to Edinburgh round trips in 24 hours. In addition, in our city, there would be subsidiary suburban passenger stations, several large goods depots on loop lines, and docks or industrial lines communicating with marshalling yards some distance away.

Practical attempts at working large through station schemes into 8ft by 7ft produced only ever decreasing circles with collieries and a few sidings and a pervasive envy of David Jenkinson's maxi-shed. Eventually I had the answer! It couldn't be done! And it would have to be a station with main, branch and parcels platforms, a 15 loco depot, a city goods depot and a 6-road marshalling yard. This sort of schizophrenic approach resulted in simultaneous exercises in measuring the loft, planning 8ft by 7ft branch lines, surveying the ⅓ acre garden and adding a suburban branch line to the other impossible list crammed into the 8ft by 7ft.

The moment of lucidity came when I closed my eyes and replayed in my mind's eye the vision of 'A4' No 19 *Bittern* drawing away from Hull Paragon station in June 1973. That was it! The railways of Hull — the most neglected city on the most neglected railway — Hull on the NER. One advantage immediately apparent is that a terminus like Hull has no restrictions on train and loco type but does not have the density of traffic of the large through station and is therefore easier to handle in model form.

**History reworked**

I turned over in my mind what might have happened north of the Humber if history, geology and geography had been slightly different. After all I would have to make some changes to get Hull into the 8ft by 7ft. If we visualise a River Hull which meanders slightly more than fact, and a city which never gained its royal charter and so remained plain, Anglo-Saxon 'Wyke', never becoming grandiose King's Town Upon Hull, we have a basis for a model railway. Wyke, a city whose docks grew large on the west side of the River Hull but whose population never climbed higher than 150,000.

The first railway was the Wyke and Ganstead, of 1840, bringing East Riding coal to the east Docks for export. The Wyke and Selby Railway was completed in 1845 with its terminus on the west side of the River Hull. This latter was the main passenger terminus in Wyke, but became inadequate as traffic increased and was inconvenient, being on the wrong side of the River Hull.

The central terminus is approached in a convoluted manner and this requires a word of explanation.

In 1880, in our personalised historical scenario, the inadequacy of the former W&S terminus and the destruction by fire of the wooden road access bridge across the mouth of the Hull, the Wyke corporation forced the NER into

**Below: Part of the original Hull Paragon station building.**
*Author*

strengthening the Hull railway bridge and expanding the former W&W terminus to its present canopied splendour. The NER directors dared not resist the corporation's scheme with its attendant expenditure, since they realised, with characteristic shrewdness, that if they did, the independent Wyke and Barnsley Railway might well be spawned and with its birth the NER monopoly in Wyke would be broken.

**Practicalities**

How to contain the main features of Wyke in a room 8ft by 7ft 4in? I did say it was impossible and so it is. The result is achieved by the logistic of 'overspill'.

As shown in the diagram, the terminus, goods depot, marshalling yard, loco depot and start of the coast/docks branch are located in the bedroom while the storage sidings are portable and spill over on to the landing. Only a modicum of angular cunning is required to make the bannister serve as a free baseboard support for the storage sidings whilst at the same time avoiding any obstruction of staircase or room access.

For baseboard supports in general I would not anticipate using the trestle or folding leg types preferring to make use of permanent fixtures on walls, door jambs etc onto which beams and baseboards would locate. The reasoning behind this is that the layout is rather introverted and designed to provide a spectacle to the operators sitting in the positions indicated. Viewed from the outside, say at an exhibition, the layout would hide all its best points and show all its worst. It is envisaged more as a permanent feature in a room with only the storage sidings being portable. Another reason for permanency of the terminus and yards is that their relative complexity and concentration of pointwork call for a very flat baseboard with the minimum of joints and with well laid and reliable trackwork. Any unreliability in a layout of this nature leads to endless frustration, not what railway modelling should be about.

For these reasons I would imagine that anyone constructing this layout, or as is more likely an adaptation of it, would run a beam or L-girder along the long wall and under the terminus, with additional supports screwed to the opposite wall and if possible build the baseboard support framework in situ. I would suggest the most sensible way of dealing with the actual baseboard surface would be to cut as much as possible, including the entire area having the greatest pointwork concentration, ie the 'window end', from a single sheet. This permanent baseboard would also provide an anchor for the hinged lifting section which permits door access when the layout is not in use.

**Track plan and operation**

A consideration of the track plan brings us to the question of gauge and scale. The plan was designed for OO gauge, 4mm/ft scale. The minimum curve radius is 24in. This occurs on the approaches to platforms 3 and 4, the curved crossover in the terminus throat and the hidden portion of the branch line. The 2ft radius would probably rule out EM gauge. Most of the remaining radii are 36in nominal, varying in practice from 34in to 41in. These radii also seem to be outside of the practical scope of P4. There is a small section of 72in/74in radius on the main line adjacent to the branch line junction. N gauge? Well, if you must, you must, but I consider it too small for serious train watching. Put your local N gauge enthusiast to the acid test. Ask him if a fat, appropriately coloured caterpillar crawled out of the tunnel, could he put his hand on his heart and say he knew instantly that it was not the railcar on the ½-hourly shuttle service? With the same space available as in OO, one would redesign the layout but retain the track radii thereby doubling the prototype equivalent. Platforms and sidings would be relatively twice as long. One could even perhaps avoid the overspill by arranging a sector plate with hidden sidings just inside the door.

O gauge or larger? Now we're talking. I would dearly love to have the space available to build this layout to 7mm/ft. But it would require 15ft by 13ft with a suitable overspill area. But just to dream of it! In 4mm scale the main restriction is in train length. We may run any train type we wish provided it does not exceed 5ft in length, excluding loco.

Wyke Central is approached by double track main line which emerges from beneath the road overbridge and sweeps around to the right, passing through 180deg before reaching the terminus. Immediately after the road bridge the main line is joined by the single track suburban/docks/industrial/coast branch from the left. Trains of various descriptions frequently creep cautiously along the branch, emerging from the overbridge, only to halt before the junction, whilst on the main line an express sweeps slowly by, decelerating for the curve and the approach to platform 1. The branch train may be the push-pull from Ganstead in which case it then trundles on to the up line before crossing over almost immediately to run wrong line on the down line for access to platforms 2 or 3. By this time passengers on the express have alighted and the station pilot removes the coaches via the curved crossover on to the down line, and then, having almost disappeared beneath the overbridge, shunts the empties back into the carriage siding.

Simultaneously, a slow freight might appear from either the branch or the main up line and take the left-hand turnout immediately after the branch junction. This train passes on to the goods reception road curving around to the right parallel with the main line. This line also doubles as the marshalling yard turnout roads though ideally there would be two separate roads. Such compromise may be unacceptable to some and could be overcome by inserting a separate goods reception road between the marshalling yard turnout road and the down main line, further complicating the pointwork at both ends and removing 2in from the platform lengths by moving the whole station layout towards the door end of the room.

The locomotive of the goods train would then be detached, and moved along the headshunt, to take water and reverse via the outside slip on to the down main line. Stopping immediately before the overbridge the loco reverses, crossing to the goods reception road and on to the back of the train which it recently brought in. Since the reception road doubles as the turnout road the newly arrived goods train blocks the turnouts and prevents shunting. This is overcome by propelling the train forward, leaving half in the headshunt and half in siding No 6. The turnouts are now clear. The train loco returns along the turnout road, perhaps as far as the headshunt behind the branch station, before reversing to the turntable and then to one of the shed roads for servicing. Meanwhile the yard pilot shunts the split goods train, taking the portion from the arrival headshunt first. Marshalling yard sidings Nos 1 to 6 would probably be used according to their destination and for my use I should label them: (1) West Yard, (2) Chemical Works, (3) East Dock, (4) Coast Branch, (5) Local, (6) Arrival. The 'local' category includes wagons destined for the goods depot, terminus, loco depot and any local industrial sidings along the branch or main lines within local trip-working distance.

A parcels train could arrive in goods reception, or platform 2, or stand on the main line between crossovers, before being shunted on to platform 4

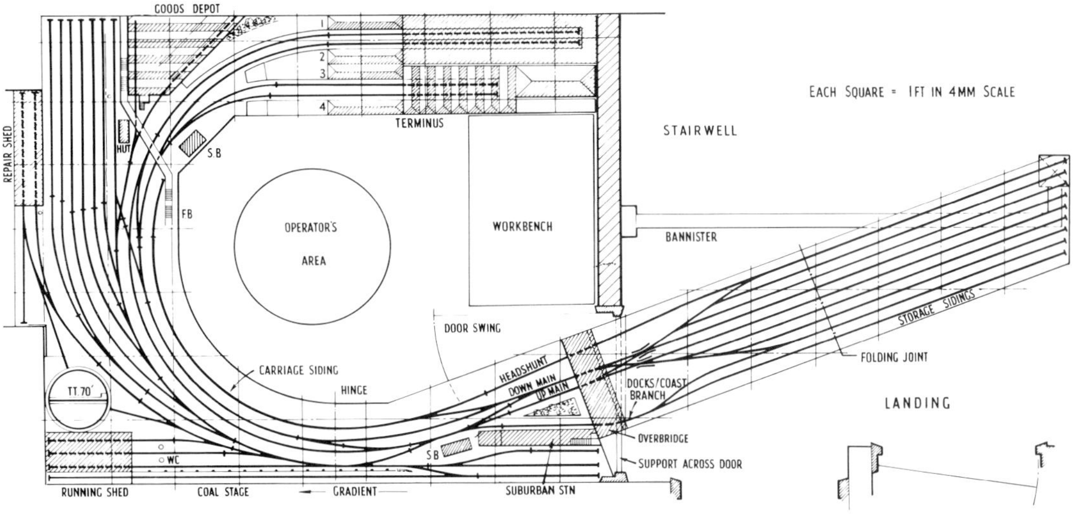

which is reserved for parcels traffic. This has dealt only with arrivals but gives an inkling of the vast operating potential, particularly in shunting, of this layout. Operating would, I consider, be most satisfying using a sequence timetable although several sessions might be necessary to complete one day's sequence.

The fiddle yard is entered through a complex of points which permit remote control and therefore single-operator working of the entire layout. If several operators could be guaranteed, a large sector table might be preferable for these storage sidings.

**Layout period and traffic balance**

The layout as drawn is suitable for modelling any period from 1910 to 1960. With modifications to the loco depot this could extend to the present day. As already stated there is no restriction on train and loco type. However, one would not expect more than two or three Pacific turns a day for post-1925 layouts. An evening through train, Pacific-hauled from Kings Cross, would be stabled overnight, returning as the early morning businessman's express to London. Likewise the fastest service to Leeds and the West Riding. Otherwise the passenger traffic would be secondary, providing main line connections at Doncaster and York, or suburban or branch line. For a modern image layout the branch line might disappear but within the city limits the suburban and docks traffic would survive.

Back in NER days coal traffic would dominate the freight, but with a healthy amount of agricultural traffic from the coast branch running through the East Riding. The docks branch provides an excuse for running any special traffic one might wish for. A feature of freight workings in a city like Wyke would be the trip working to local industry and the transfer freights between various yards within the city. The long curve is not apparent to the operator since he sits at the centre of curvature and the train remains at the same distance from him throughout its time on the curve. The curvature also closes up the gaps between coaches and wagons. Sitting in the operator's position all that can be seen is a succession of NER or ex-NER trains going about their business efficiently amid ex-NER lineside features on acres of track. Heaven!

I only hope that one day the NER really does triumph and I can report having built the layout.

**Below: Hull Dairycoates west box in 1974.** *Author*

# Small Structures 4

# SR pre-cast concrete platforms

From the late 1920s onwards the Southern Railway made extensive use of pre-cast concrete components for its stations and lineside structures. Station platforms built from pre-cast concrete components first appeared on the SR in the mid-1920s and the extensive programme of station reconstruction in connection with electrification led to the appearance of the new platforms all over the SR systems. They were used for new construction and also for extending existing platforms and completely replaced traditional brick construction. To complement the pre-cast platforms the SR produced lamp posts, station nameboards and even solid-panel concrete fencing. So widespread was the use of these items, that many still survive today, although the numbers of concrete nameboards and lamps are steadily reducing.

The platforms consisted of concrete frame sections spaced at 4ft centres, with solid facing panels which slotted in between them. In some positions, where the platform was above ground level, the frames were used without the facing panels, but otherwise the platform frame and

**Below: Watergate halt on the North Devon & Cornwall Junction Railway, taken in 1966.** *B. Quemby*

WATERGATE
20

facing would be back-filled. The surface could be either gravel, or more usually asphalt, with the edge formed of 3ft by 4ft concrete slabs.

The drawing depicts a rather unusual application of the design, as it was used for two rural halts, Yarde and Watergate, on the North Devon and Cornwall Junction line between Halwill Junction and Torrington. Half the total platform length has been drawn, the lamp, platform and ramp on the other half being a mirror image. There was just one noticeboard and nameboard placed as shown in the drawing. The tilley lamp post and nameboards were concrete, but the notice board posts appear to have been timber. The 'spur' at the base of the tilley lamp posts, was a timber step to enable railway staff to reach the hook. Below the hook was a metal ring to stop the lamp swinging.

**Left: Watergate halt.** *B. Quemby*

**Below: Extension to a main line station using pre-cast parts.** *IA Library*

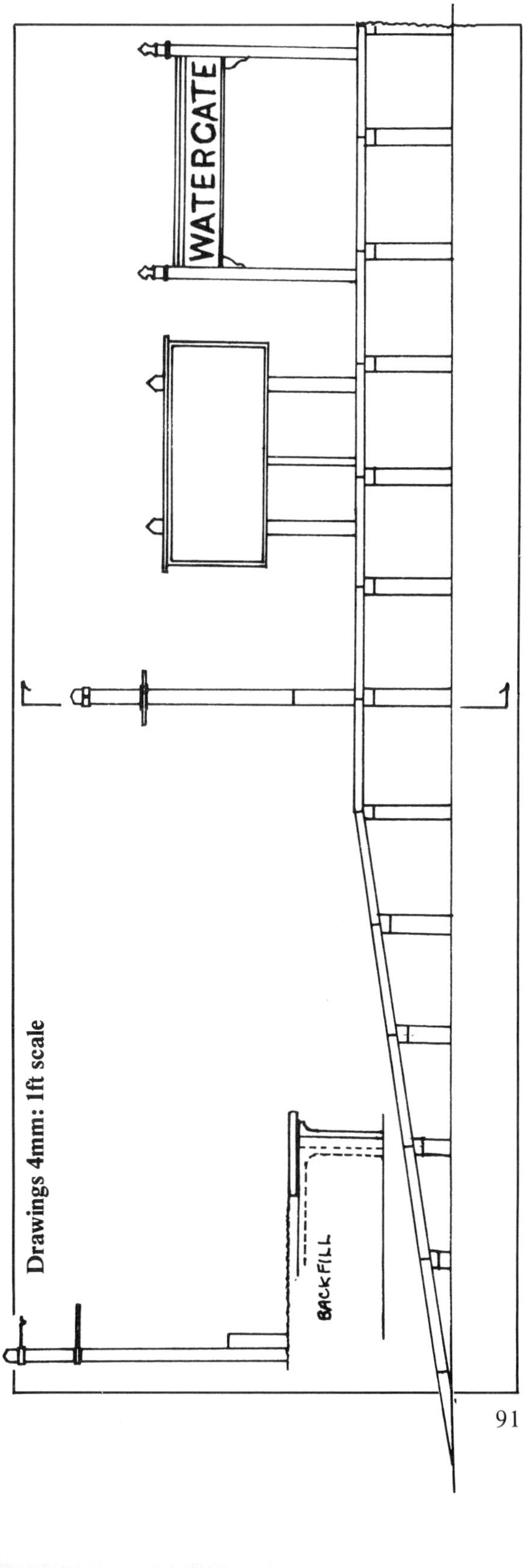

# BR Plate Wagons and some related conversions

*Paul W. Bartlett* BSc & *Trevor Mann* BA

(British Railways Historical Study Group)
(Historical Model Railway Society)

Long, low, drop-sided wagons for the carriage of plate steel had their origins on the pre-grouping railways. Later, the LNER and LMS built many such wagons, initially with wooden bodies, but, from 1937 and 1944 respectively, using riveted steel construction. As with some other wagon types these 'rival' companies adopted similar designs and both called them 'PLATE' wagons. By nationalisation both companies were building these wagons using either riveting or welding for the construction of the ends and welding only for the sides. In addition the LNER had built 250 wagons with a vacuum clasp braked underframe. Both companies also used a similar, non-vacuum brake design, with the addition of a pair of bolsters, as convertible double-bolster wagons.

British Railways continued to build substantially similar designs. They quickly produced 400 double-bolsters numbered B920000-920339. These are mentioned here to avoid confusion but they do not form part of this article. The Plates were much more numerous and varied. They were built up to 1961, by which time no less than 6,568 wagons had been completed, of which 43 were built new for the Signalling and Telecommunications Engineers (S&T) and numbered in the departmental fleet.

Subsequently this early demonstration of the versatility of the design has been recognised frequently and various adaptions, rebuilds and re-uses have been found during the intervening years. These BR built Plates and some of the conversions are the subject of this article.

**The Plates**

The weight diagrams 1/430 and 1/431 are very similar, the main differences being that the solebar of 1/431 is $\frac{1}{4}''$ higher than that of 1/430. These diagrams are illustrated by Fig 1 and Photograph 1. The bodies of these wagons were

**Below: Diagram 1/431 Plate No B932149, with rivetted ends and welded sides. It has a non-fitted RCH long-link underframe with BR one-piece axleboxes, plate axleguards and four-web buffers.** *P. W. Bartlett*

1

**Fig 1**

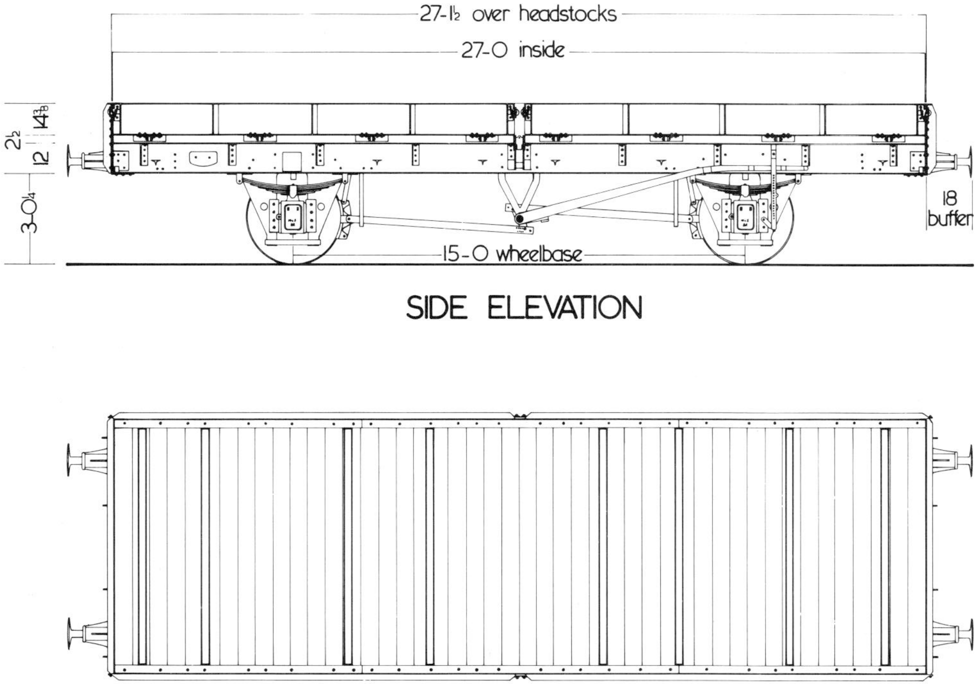


SIDE ELEVATION

PLAN

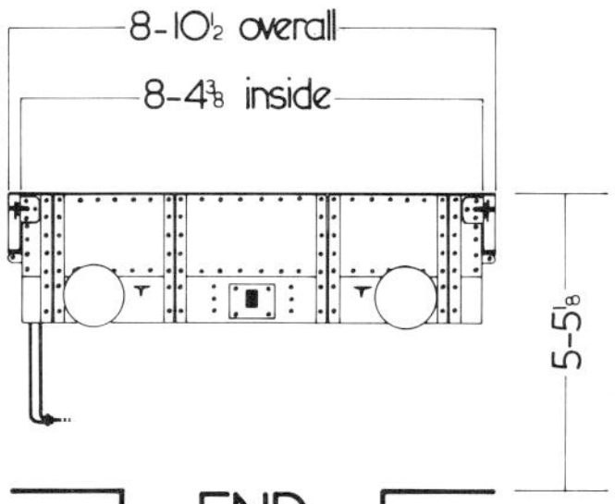


END ELEVATION

Drawn from measurements taken from B 932550 at Manningtree, 7/81.

Variations occur in buffers, couplings and axleboxes. Diagram 1/430 wagons are identical to diagram 1/431 vehicles except for a decrease of ¼ inch in height from rail to bottom of solebar and in total height. Wagons built to Lot 2151 only have all-welded ends.

| |
|---|
| B.R.H.S.G. |
| British Railways 22 ton Plate Wagon (non-fitted). Diagram 1/431 |
| T.J. Mann ©1981 |
| WD 1-431 TM |

*All drawings 4mm:1 ft scale*

2

3

all-steel and the sides were of welded fabricated construction which formed two drop-doors with a removable central stanchion between. The ends were fixed in place, and of either riveted or welded construction. We have observed specific end types for each lot but it may be that each lot had vehicles with both welded and riveted ends. The floors were cross-planked and the plank ends were plated over where they would be exposed on the sides. These wagons lacked continuous brakes, having one brake per wheel connected across the wagon. The wheelbase was 15ft and they were 27ft $1\frac{1}{2}$in over headstocks. The axleguards were varied, being either of the open RCH pattern or the solid plate type. B930330 had an example of each when seen in 1977. Similarly the axleboxes were either of the LMS or RCH 2-piece type or the LNER or BR 1-piece type. Later roller bearings were sometimes fitted. Normally three hole disc wheels were fitted but occasionally spoked wheels were used in replacement.

The capital-stock wagons normally had a grey body with black underframes throughout their

4

**Above left: A diagram 1/430 Winkle No KDB 997511 built in 1951 at Shildon to Lot 2201. Body and underframe details are the same as previous illustration, but the vehicle is painted black.** *P. W. Bartlett*

**Left: Shildon-built (1957) diagram 1/432 Plate No B933525. The body has rivetted ends and welded sides on an LNER clasp vacuum brake underframe with BR one-piece axleboxes, plate axleguards and side-web buffers. Body painted bauxite, underframe, black.** *P. W. Bartlett*

**Above: Diagram 1/434 Plate No B935743 built 1960. Welded body sides and ends on BR clasp vacuum brake underframe with Athermos roller bearings, plate axleguards and replacement Oleo-pneumatic buffers in unpainted green undercoat.**

lives. The lettering was white on a black panel, but after 1964 it was outlined in boxes in the style introduced by the corporate image. The code 'PLATE' was always carried near the number panel until replaced by the TOPS code 'SPO'. This was introduced in 1977. This system coincided with most of these wagons being taken out of use and stored at large marshalling yards. For example, many hundreds were stored at Whitemoor, Cambridgeshire until extensive scrapping began towards the end of 1980. Now, the only wagons of these diagrams which remain in service are those used by the engineers and some vacuum braked conversions of 1/431. The engineers also still have their own fleet of S&T Plates. These were originally code named 'WINKLE' and now, under TOPS, are coded 'ZVO'. Photograph 2 shows one of these. Often these wagons carry lettering which indicates the job to which they are allocated. For example, KDB997507 has 'S&T CHESTER, KDB997511 has 'RETURN TO ST STORE CENTRE SIDING BLETCHLEY', KDB997525 has 'S&T KENTISH TOWN LONDON MIDLAND'. These wagons had black bodies and underframes with white lettering when introduced and all those observed have continued to have this style.

Thus, by 1956 BR had constructed 2,868 of these non-continuous braked Plates. Thereafter the implementation of the 1955 Modernisation Plan required all future construction to have continuous vacuum brake.

The first of the vacuum braked 'Plates' of BR diagram 1/432 are particularly interesting in that they returned to an LNER design, as they all have the characteristic LNER vacuum clasp-brake underframe with two acute V-hangers on one side and only a single V-hanger on the other side. The vacuum cylinder is offset to this side. Fig 2 and Photograph 3 illustrate this type. The body and underframe details are more settled in this design as the sides are always welded and the ends always of riveted construction. Many of lot 2734 and all of lots 2862 and 3128 have four, butterfly-wing shaped cleats as roping points on each side. These are attached to the plating which covers the floor ends. Most of these wagons appear to have been introduced with 1-piece axleboxes, and some were interestingly, of the typical LNER slope-fronted design. In addition a few of these wagons had 2-piece axleboxes and some received isothermos or roller-bearing axleboxes as replacements. Painting and lettering of these is the same as discussed later for diagram 1/434. Altogether 1,200 wagons of the LNER design were built.

The final Plate diagram, 1/434, had a new design of vacuum clasp-braked underframe which had an asymmetric brake hanger. Photograph 4 shows this design. Two lots of these were built from new, totalling 2,500 wagons. The bodies of these were all-welded and they also had plate axleguards. Many of lot 3223 were built with isothermos axleboxes and some of lot 3338 also received these. The remainder all had roller bearings. In addition to these wagons many diagram 1/431 wagons were converted to the same arrangement of vacuum clasp-brake underframe (see Photograph 5.) Examples of this conversion are B931397, B931465, B931626, B931682, B932073, B932314 and B932522.

All of the vacuum-braked Plates had bauxite bodies with black underframes. The lettering was white, and after 1964 it was outlined in white boxes. They carried the code name 'PLATE VB' until after 1977, when the TOPS code 'SPV' replaced this.

Plate wagons were versatile. Apart from their use for steel traffic they carried many other goods. Examples are farm implements and vehicles — particularly military ones such as Landrovers, cars and ammunition-carrying trailers. In 1968 large boulders were carried from the Peak District for the deep-water harbour at Port Talbot and similarly, from the mid 1970s many were carried to Angerstein wharf for the Thames flood barrier. Also at this time narrow gauge bogies (for wagons ordered by African railways) were carried from Gloucester to BREL workshops and to the docks.

This versatility extended to the many other uses to which Plates were put. These uses required lesser or greater conversion, and some of these are described in the following notes.

### Condor Conflats

One series of conversions involved the 'Condor' Conflat Ps introduced in 1959. These were originally allocated diagram number 1/433, but

**Below: A 1951 diagram 1/431 Plate which has been converted to vacuum brake with BR clasp underframe, Athermos axleboxes, RCH axleguards and Oleo-pneumatic buffers.**

5

Fig 2

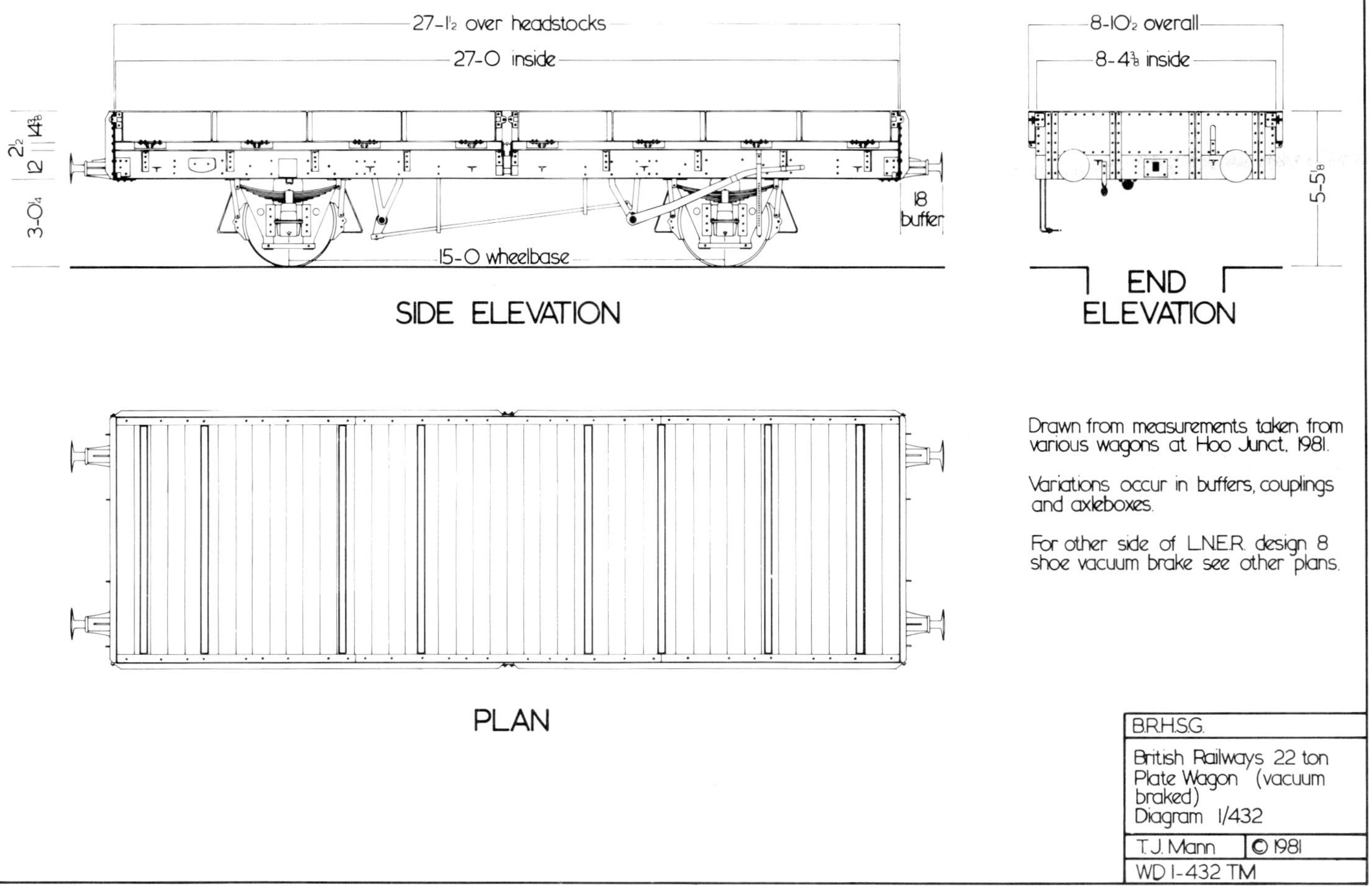
27-1½ over headstocks
27-0 inside
2½
14⅜
12
3-0¼
18 buffer
15-0 wheelbase
SIDE ELEVATION
8-10½ overall
8-4⅜ inside
5-5⅛
END ELEVATION
PLAN
Drawn from measurements taken from various wagons at Hoo Junct. 1981.
Variations occur in buffers, couplings and axleboxes.
For other side of L.N.E.R. design 8 shoe vacuum brake see other plans.
B.R.H.S.G.
British Railways 22 ton Plate Wagon (vacuum braked)
Diagram 1/432
T.J. Mann
© 1981
WD 1-432 TM

6

**Above: 'Condor' Conflat P No B933273 being loaded with a 4 ton A-type container at Hendon. The open deck, locating corners, crossbar, shackles and original end can all be seen. The wagon has LNER clasp vacuum brake underframe, eye bolt suspension, SKF roller bearings, Dowty pneumatic buffers and plate axleguards.**
*British Railways*

this was quickly reallocated number 1/60. The official diagram reproduced as Fig 3 and the official Photograph (6) showing loading at Hendon, illustrate the main features of the design. The wagons were converted from vacuum clasp-braked members of diagram 1/431 (examples are B931614 and B932775) and from diagram 1/432 with the LNER clasp-brake underframe (examples are B932869, B932944/5, B932956, B933061, B933182, B933417, B933670 and B933861). The sides and floors were removed to leave the plate ends and the exposed girders of the underframe. This makes them reminiscent of the LMS 'conflat' chassis of 1932. A girder runs across the wagon about one third of the way along and simple, container locating, corners are positioned on either side of this girder and at each corner of the wagon. These prevent the containers moving sideways or lengthways. Chains and shackles are located beside each of the container locating corners. Additional alterations are that the solebar is 12" deep rather than 10" deep at all but its extreme ends (the headstocks remain 10in deep) and that all are fitted with roller-bearings and auxiliary rubber eye-bolt suspension (commonly called J-hanger).

These 'Conflat Ps' were used for a new and important concept of freight train. Each wagon was able to carry one A-type and one B-type standard container. They ran as block trains between Hendon, London and Gushetfaulds, Glasgow, taking the Midland mainline and the Settle and Carlisle route.

They were often hauled by pairs of the new Metro-Vick Co-Bo diesels and one of the trains

Fig 3

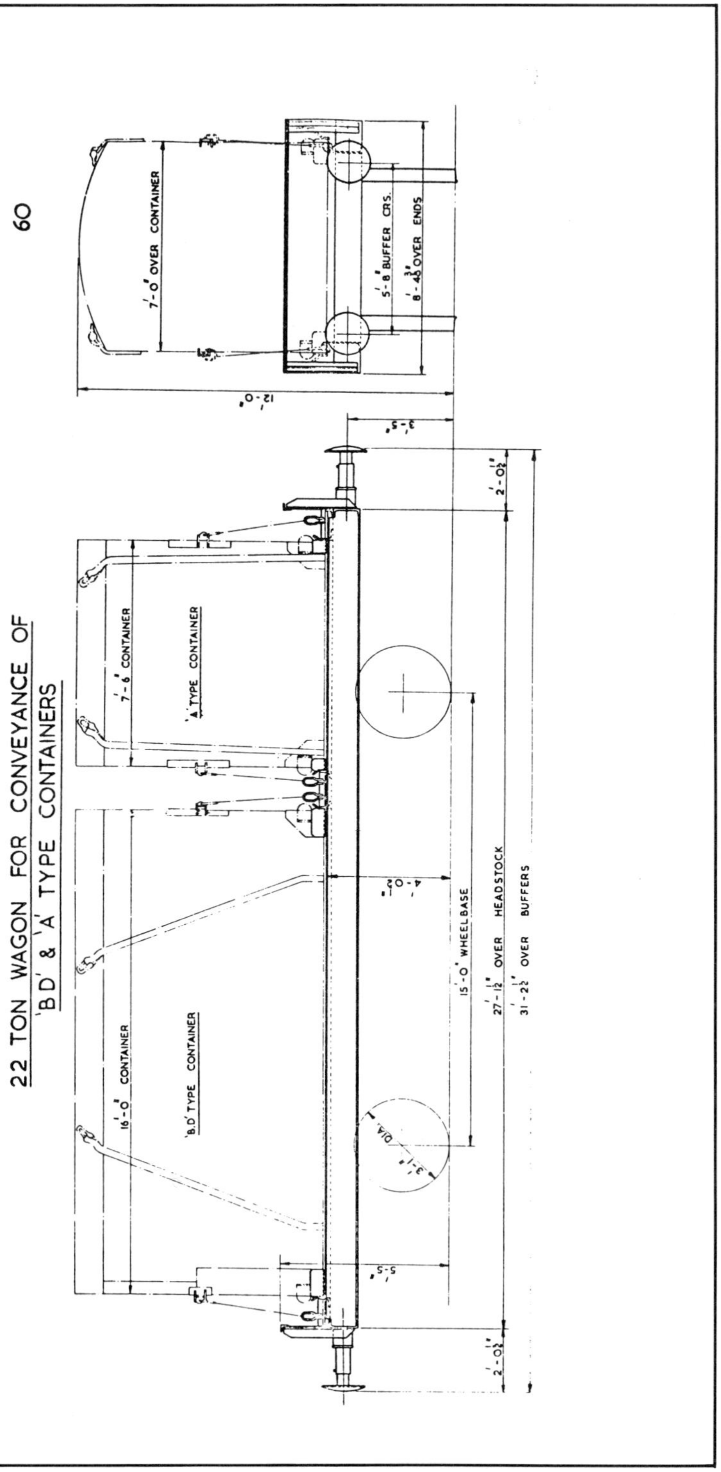
22 TON WAGON FOR CONVEYANCE OF
'B D' & 'A' TYPE CONTAINERS
16'-0" CONTAINER
'B.D' TYPE CONTAINER
7'-6" CONTAINER
'A' TYPE CONTAINER
15'-0" WHEELBASE
27'-1½" OVER HEADSTOCK
31'-2½" OVER BUFFERS
2'-0½"
3'-5"
12'-0"
60
7'-0" OVER CONTAINER
5'-8" BUFFER CRS.
8'-4⅜" OVER ENDS
3'-1" DIA.

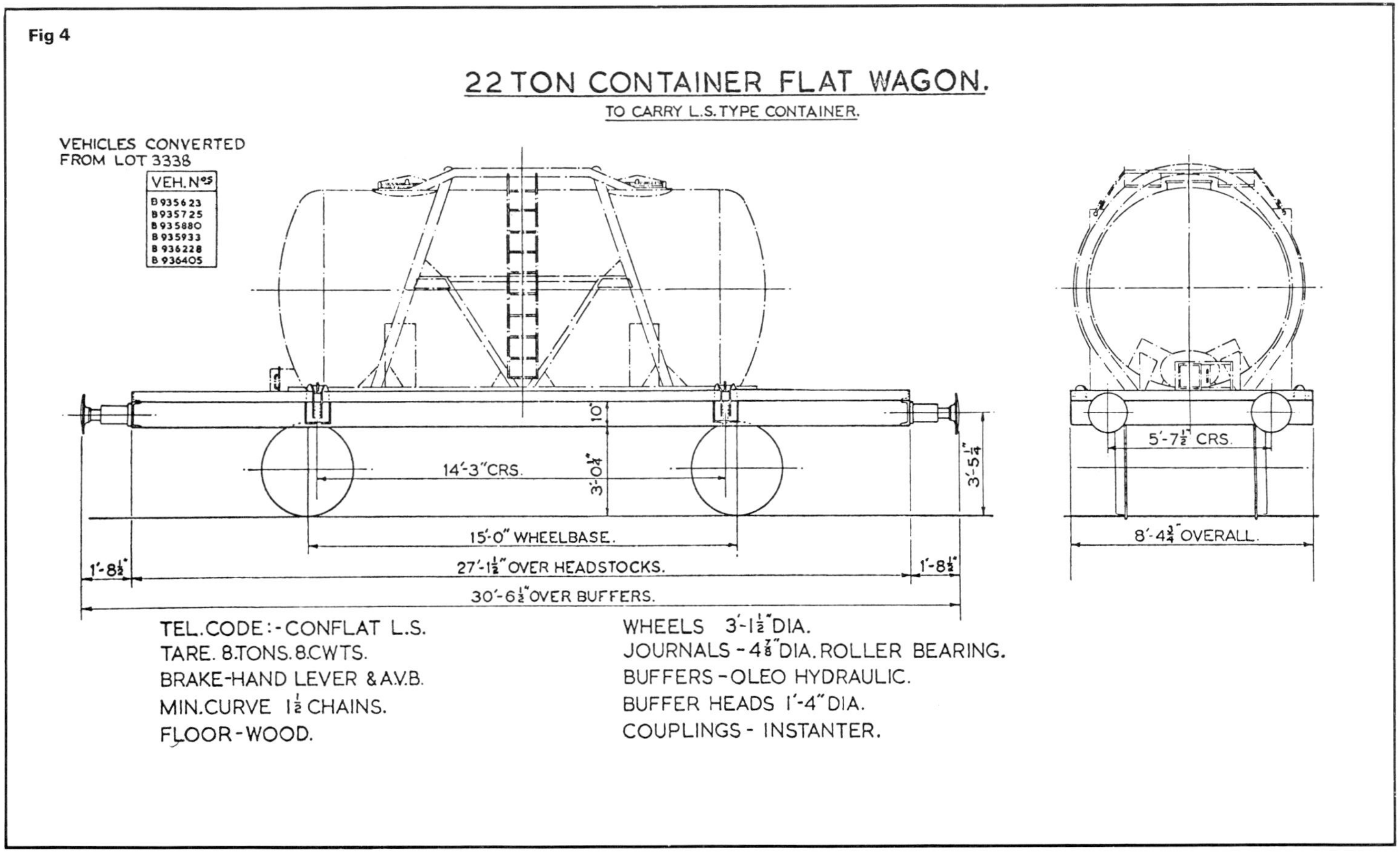
22 TON CONTAINER FLAT WAGON.
TO CARRY L.S. TYPE CONTAINER.
VEHICLES CONVERTED FROM LOT 3338
VEH. N^os
B 935623
B 935725
B 935880
B 935933
B 936228
B 936405
10"
14'-3" CRS.
3'-0¼"
3'-5¼"
15'-0" WHEELBASE.
1'-8½"
27'-1½" OVER HEADSTOCKS.
1'-8½"
30'-6½" OVER BUFFERS.
5'-7½" CRS.
8'-4¾" OVERALL.
TEL. CODE:- CONFLAT L.S.
TARE. 8 TONS. 8 CWTS.
BRAKE-HAND LEVER & A.V.B.
MIN. CURVE 1½ CHAINS.
FLOOR-WOOD.
WHEELS 3'-1½" DIA.
JOURNALS - 4⅞" DIA. ROLLER BEARING.
BUFFERS - OLEO HYDRAULIC.
BUFFER HEADS 1'-4" DIA.
COUPLINGS - INSTANTER.

Fig 4

Fig 5

## 22TON CONFLAT 'P' FOR I.S.O. CONTAINERS
(CONVERTED FROM DIAGRAM PAGE 60)

B.R. 1/121

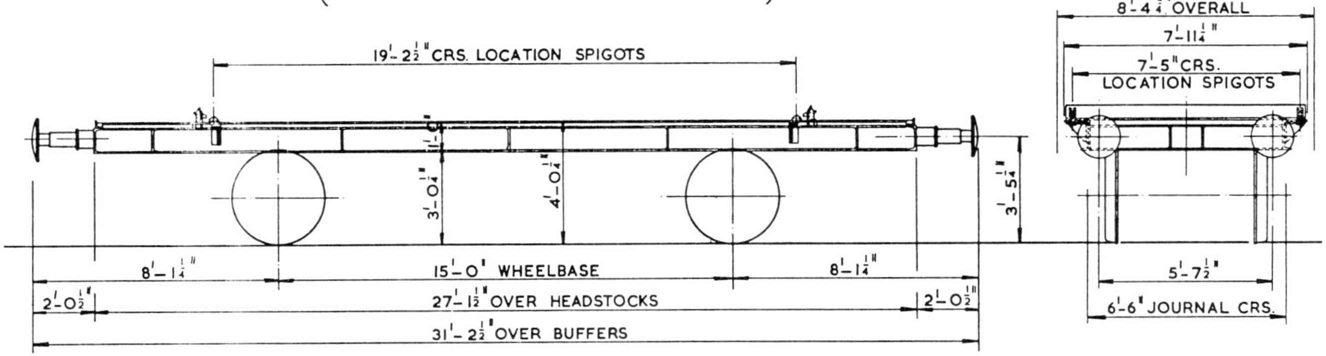


TYPE CODE - CONFLAT P
MINIMUM CURVE - 1½ CHAIN
TARE - 8 TON 2 CWT
CARRYING CAPACITY - 22 TON
MAX. SPEED - 50 M.P.H. LOADED
TYPE OF BRAKE - A.V.B. (CLASP) & HAND LEVER

SPRINGS - LAMINATED
SUSPENSION - EYEBOLT
WHEELS - 3FT. 1IN. DIA.
JOURNALS - 4⅞ INS. DIA. ROLLER BEARINGS
BUFFERS - HYDRAULIC
BUFFER HEADS - 1FT. 4INS. DIA.
COUPLINGS - INTERNATIONAL SCREW

| QTY | VEHICLE NUMBERS |
|---|---|
| 8 | B 933090, 933221, 933289, 933750, 933846, 935594, 935915, 936368 |

VEHICLES NOT TO BE LOOSE SHUNTED

used No M32921M, an LMS 6-wheel 'stove' parcels van (diagram 1796) as a brake van. They were replaced by bogie 'Conflat Es' during 1964 which in turn were replaced by the earliest Freightliner container trains. So, the revolution they heralded had quickly caught up with them. Instead of releasing them to general container service (the containers they were designed to carry lasted until 1977) they were stored at Hendon until conversion to Timber Ps (see below).

**Other Conflat Conversions**

'Plates' also formed the basis of other 'Conflats' for special uses. Four of these conversions are known to us, but there may well have been others.

The six 'Conflat LS' carried 'LS' type containers and were numbered B935623, B935725, B935880, B935933, B936228, and B936405. Diagram 1/78 of these is shown as Fig 4. There were 15 'LS' tank-type containers, LS19984B-19998B of diagram 3/455 which were built in 1962. The 'Conflat LS' differed from the Condor 'Conflat P' in not having raised ends or eye-bolt suspension and in only carrying a single container located at 14′ 3″ centres. These wagons were also converted to Timber Ps and would seem to have been very short-lived as 'Conflats'.

We know less about the next conversion. In the BTC magazine *Transport Age* (No 21 of April 1962) there is a photograph of No B933620 loaded with 2 'LG' containers. 14 'LG' containers were built in about 1960 and allocated diagram 3/451. These carried 6 tons of bulk grain which was loaded through a pair of roof hatches and unloaded, by gravity, through a pair of shutes on the side. We know of no diagram for this Conflat, which we assume was called 'Conflat LG'. This conversion retained the chassis and timber floor. The original sides and ends were removed and replaced by a low side and end. The sides were cut down at the position of the container side unloading shutes. There was also a low batten (possibly two) running across the floor of the wagon to help to hold the containers in position. It is likely that there were several more of this design of Conflat and that they would have had a black underframe and bauxite body with the pre-1964 lettering style. The containers would have been maroon with straw-coloured lettering.

The fourth Conflat conversion was from the Condor 'Conflat Ps' and, to add to the confusion, were also code named 'Conflat P'. They were designed to carry 20ft ISO containers and were probably introduced in 1964 or 1965. Their diagram 1/121 is reproduced as Figure 5. The eight wagons, B933090, B933221, B933289, B933750, B933846, B935594, B935915 and B936368 lost their ends but retained the eye-bolt suspension. We do not know any further details about these wagons, neither do we know how successful they were. ISO type box containers have an 8ft by 8ft profile which usually fouls the loading gauge when loaded at a normal height. Because of this 100 Lowmacs were converted to carry ISO containers and, later of course, Freightliner chassis were introduced with wheels of smaller diameter than is normal. It is possible that these 'Conflat Ps' may have been used for some special containers such as opens or Lancashire flats.

The final container-carrying conversion is more modern but as we have not observed the wagons we do not have complete details of them. Five 'Plates', B934398, B935416, B935653, B935793 and B936129 are TOPS — coded 'FPB' and in 1981 were being used to carry coal in containers between Bow Hill Washeries and Elgin. These were converted from diagram 1/434 to 1/466 by removal of the vacuum brakes (although the vacuum through pipes were retained) and the fitting of airbrakes. In addition the underframe was modified by being fitted with single long link suspension so that the maximum speed could be raised to 75mph. BR converted small numbers of many of its standard wagon designs to airbrake in 1969, as experiments, and it is most likely that these were converted at this time. We do not know what body modifications have subsequently been made for their present role. However, as they share the Pool with an ex 'SAA', a 2-axle steel carrier (Steel AB) which has never had any sides it is possible that the sides of the 'Plates' have been removed.

**Timber P**

The 'Timber Ps' were introduced in mid 1965 for the transport of rough timber logs from a railhead at Crianlarich to the pulp mill at Corpach on the West Highland line. Fig 6 and Photograph 7 which BR allocated diagram 1/439 show the Timber P. The conversion was described and

Fig 6

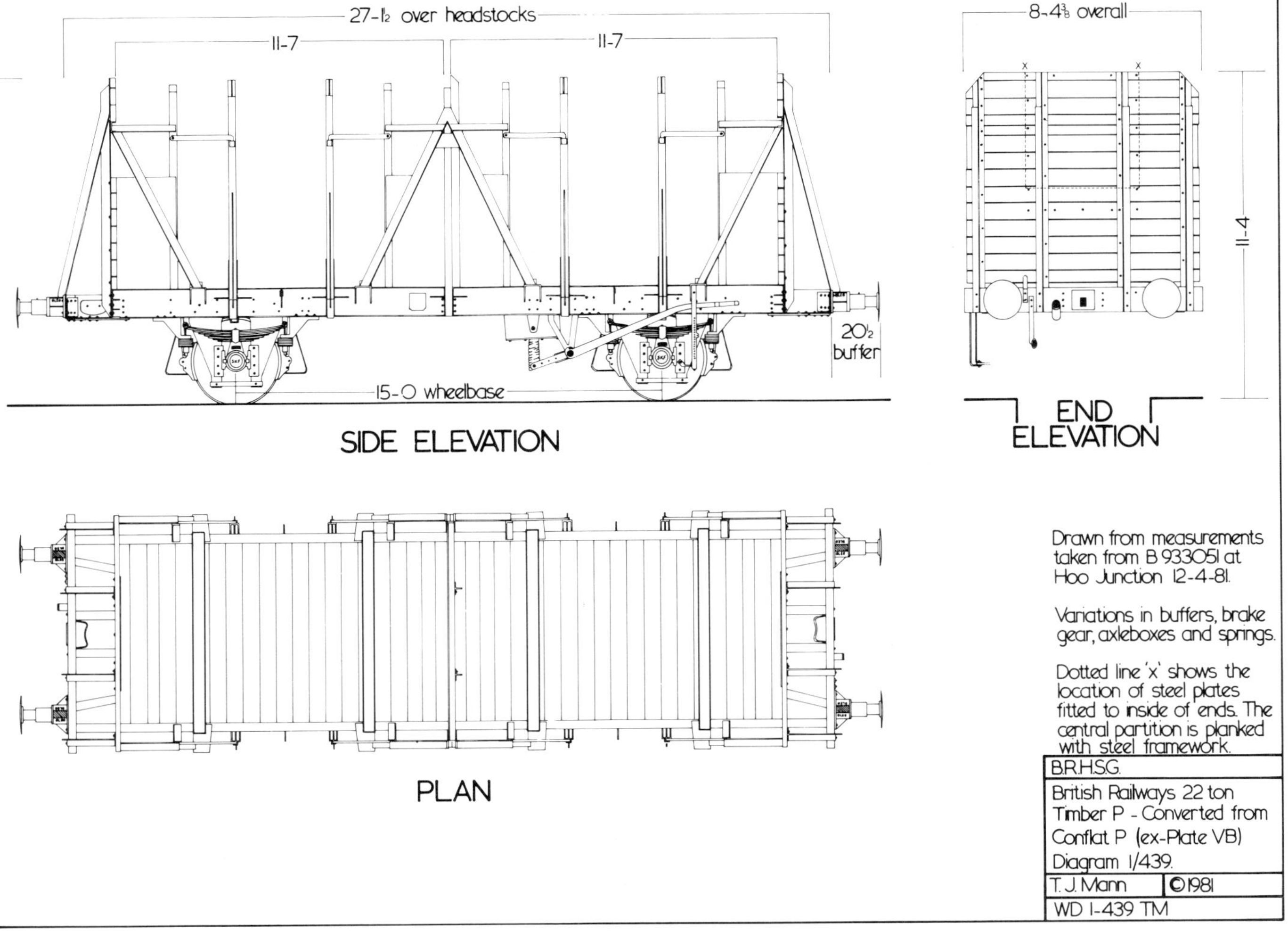
27-1½ over headstocks
11-7
11-7
7-4
12
3-0
20½ buffer
15-0 wheelbase
SIDE ELEVATION
8-4⅜ overall
11-4
END ELEVATION
PLAN
Drawn from measurements taken from B 933051 at Hoo Junction 12-4-81.
Variations in buffers, brake gear, axleboxes and springs.
Dotted line 'x' shows the location of steel plates fitted to inside of ends. The central partition is planked with steel framework.
B.R.H.S.G.
British Railways 22 ton Timber P - Converted from Conflat P (ex-Plate VB) Diagram 1/439.
T. J. Mann
©1981
WD 1-439 TM

7

**Above: Timber P conversion of vacuum-fitted, roller bearing, Plate underframe being painted after conversion at Barassie Works, in April 1965. The body is bauxite with white lettering and the underframe is black.**
*British Railways*

**Left: Loaded and empty Timber P conversions at Crianlarich in July 1970. They were used to supply a pulp mill at Corpach.** *British Railways*

illustrated in *Modern Railways*, (June 1965). *Modern Railways* talks of 50 wagons being converted at Barassie works from Condor 'Conflat Ps'. We know of 37 'Conflat Ps' converted to 'Timber P' which retain the eye-bolt suspension, together with six 'Conflat LS' and B935725 (we do not know the origin of this wagon) without eye-bolt suspension. There may have been additional 'Timber Ps' but we have no details. The wagons, which continued to carry the same 'Plate'-series numbers, retained little more than the original underframe with vacuum brake and roller bearings. High planked ends and planked centre panels were built on, battens fitted across the floor and open girder work on the side.

The results were high capacity wagons which

8

**Above: Experimental 10 ton demountable petrol tank on ex-Plate underframe No B936413 which has BR clasp vacuum brake, roller bearings, plate axleguards and Oleo-pneumatic buffers.** *British Railways*

were intensively used until severe financial retrenchment at the pulp works during 1981 resulted in the loss of the traffic and scrapping of the wagons.

**Demountable Petrol Tank**

The next conversion is the demountable petrol tank introduced in 1964, No B936413. This is not unlike a 'Conflat' but is rather more interesting in some respects. Photograph 8 shows the wagon and further photographs and explanation are to be found in *Transport Age* (No 31 of December 1964). The 'Plate' chassis has BR vacuum clasp brake and lowered decking, with the top of the solebar proud of the deck and three pairs of conical mountings. These are used to locate and lock the tank in position. The tank, built by Darham Industries Ltd, has an unusual cross-section and a long narrow container on either side where the pipes used during unloading of the petrol are kept. A Lancer side loader fork truck lifted the tank on to a Foden lorry chassis which also had the three pairs of conical mountings. The idea behind this design was to load at a refinery railhead, tranship the tank at a rail depot to the road vehicle for onward delivery to a petrol station, without intermediate unloading of the petrol.

The wagon was attractively painted in the standard livery for light fuel oil wagons. The running gear and buffer beams were black, the solebars were red with white lettering and a pair of fast traffic stars. The tank was silver with black lettering. Nothing more came of this interesting experiment and no form of containerisation has become common for fuel oils although the wagon and tank still exist. It is now in the departmental fleet and is used for storage in the sidings adjacent to the research laboratories at Derby. It is now painted entirely black.

**Reach Wagons**

Perhaps the simplest conversions are to reach wagons. These are used in front of a locomotive

9

**Above: A diagram 1/434 Plate No B934769 converted to an under-runner with ends removed and sides laid flat on the floor. It has BR clasp vacuum brake underframe, Hybox roller bearings, plate axleguards and replacement Oleo-pneumatic buffers. The vehicle is largely unpainted and rusty.** *P. W. Bartlett*

to reach safely in to a fuel oil or petrol loading or unloading bay to correctly place the tank wagons. The 'Plate' bodies are unmodified, they do not have continuous brakes but, instead have been fitted with through pipes for both vacuum and air brake. Each is allocated to a particular depot, but sometimes they can be seen long distances from these. Because the wagons are allocated to the non-revenue earning traffic fleet of departmental wagons they are prefixed TD. Each wagon is lettered with is location, examples are TDB931631 'REACH WAGON WEST THURROCK ER', TDB931716 'REACH WAGON HAWKESBURY LANE LMR', TDB931937 'REACH WAGON HUNSLET LANE ER'.

### Runner Wagons

Another simple conversion, which was introduced during 1979 was to 'runner' wagons. The ends are cut off and the sides are unbolted and then placed flat on the now exposed floor. This leaves a low flat wagon of about 9 tonnes tare. These wagons are used as under runners for wagons with long loads of steel. They work usually with Bogie Bolsters, especially 'Ds' loaded with new rail from the BSC works at Workington. Photograph 9 of B934019 shows a wagon used in this way. Other examples are B934141, B934242, B934289, B934601, B934769, B935037 and B935755. They are TOPS-coded 'RRV'.

This design is an example of history repeating itself. The LNER introduced some very similar, vacuum braked, 'FLAT' wagons in 1939, although these lacked the extra weight given by the old sides.

## COILS

Over the years BR has accumulated a varied fleet of 'coil' wagons. These carry coiled steel strip or coiled steel rod, two rather different commodities which require quite different loading and handling. Many of the 'coils' are conversions of other wagons and the 'Plates' have been the basis for at least four of these.

### Coil D

From the mid-1960's 'Coil Ds' were converted to work from Rotherham, carrying 7 ton loads of coiled steel strip in three demountable cradles.

**Fig 7**

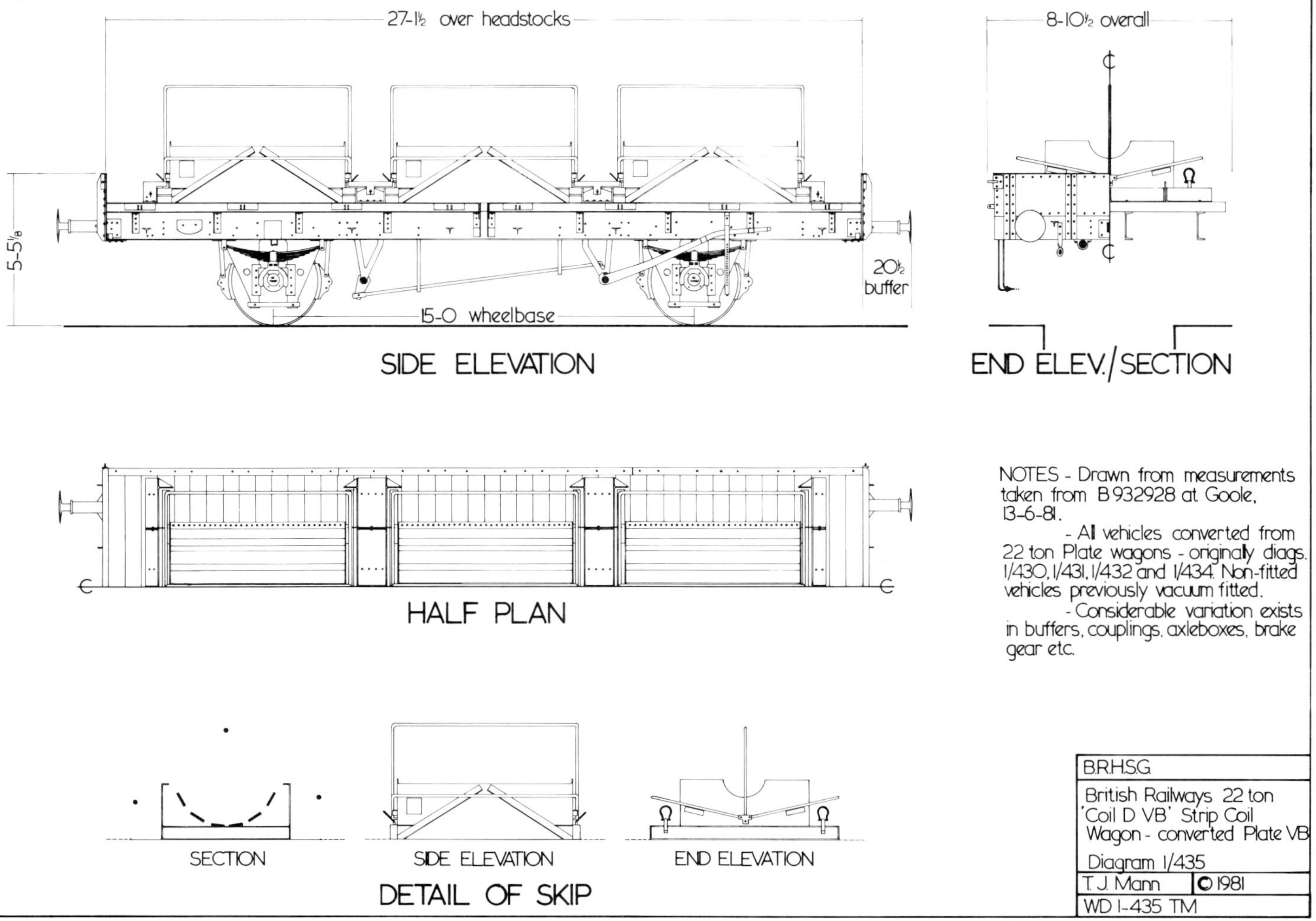
27-1½ over headstocks
5-5⅛
15-0 wheelbase
20½ buffer
SIDE ELEVATION
8-10½ overall
END ELEV./SECTION
HALF PLAN
NOTES - Drawn from measurements taken from B 932928 at Goole, 13-6-81.
- All vehicles converted from 22 ton Plate wagons - originally diags. 1/430, 1/431, 1/432 and 1/434. Non-fitted vehicles previously vacuum fitted.
- Considerable variation exists in buffers, couplings, axleboxes, brake gear etc.
SECTION
SIDE ELEVATION
END ELEVATION
DETAIL OF SKIP
B.R.H.S.G.
British Railways 22 ton 'Coil D VB' Strip Coil Wagon - converted Plate VB
Diagram 1/435
T. J. Mann
© 1981
WD 1-435 TM

Diagram 1/435 was allocated to the 71 wagons and shows the wagons with sides, but unidentified 'Coil Ds' seen in October 1966 did not have sides. Thus the illustrations Fig 7 and Photograph 10 are more representative of the wagons in traffic. The original 'Plate' end and floor was retained and they all had roller bearings and vacuum brake. The cradles were mounted length-wise on the chassis. An individual hood supported by three metal hoops protected the steel; the hoops folded sideways when the coils were being unloaded. Each cradle was bauxite and was separately lettered 'BRITISH RAIL COIL D VB Return to Rotherham'. Each was individually numbered.

At some stage three were reconverted to Plates — B931531, B932115 and B933001. B932007 was converted to a 'Coil E' (see below) and 26 were converted to 'Coil R' (see below) including B935252, B935401, B935508, B936507. All of the remaining 'Coil Ds' were scrapped during the summer of 1981 including B931095, B931188, B932253, B933055 and B936328. They were coded 'KDV' on TOPS.

**Coil F**

A similar design to the 'Coil D' is the 25 'Coil Fs' ('KFV' on TOPS) as they also have demountable cradles for coiled strip steel. They worked from South Wales mainly to the Midlands. Diagram 1/424 was issued for this conversion in the 1960s which is illustrated by Fig 8 and Photograph 11. The ends, floor and roller bearing vacuum-braked underframe remain from the 'Plates'. Four cradles are mounted crosswise. Each was originally hooded but these were mostly removed by the mid 1970s. The cradles were bauxite with white lettering which read 'COILS TO BE LOADED WITH LOOSE END AWAY FROM HOOD LOAD & TARE NOT TO EXCEED 6 TONS.' This fleet was converted from a mixture of diagrams 1/431, 1/432, and 1/434; examples were B931170, B931368, B931653, B932767, B933458, B935459 and B936358. They were all withdrawn during the summer of 1981.

**Below: Coil D VB No B932928 ex-diagram 1/432. It has LNER clasp brake underframe, roller bearings, plate axleguards and web buffers. At Goole docks on 4 May 1981.** *R. Silsbury*

**Bottom: Coil F (now KFV) No B936516 ex-diagram 1/434. It has BR clasp brake underframe, roller bearings, plate axleguards and Oleo-pneumatic buffers. At Newport on 12 July 1978.** *R. Silsbury*

10

11

Fig 8

# 24 TON STRIP COIL WAGON

## EX 22 TON PLATE WAGON

| LETTERED | TELE CODE | LOT № | QTY | VEH. № |
|---|---|---|---|---|
| COIL F | COIL F | PART 2199<br>PART 2327<br>PART 2476<br>PART 2604<br>PART 2734<br>PART 2862<br>PART 3223<br><br><br>PART 3338 | 25 | B931170 B931368<br>B931653<br>B931832<br>B932767<br>B933286<br>B933456<br>B935247 B935321 B935335<br>B935343 B935404 B935440<br>B935459 B935464<br>B935734 B935815 B935929<br>B936045 B936063 B936234<br>B936318 B936357 B936358<br>B936516 |

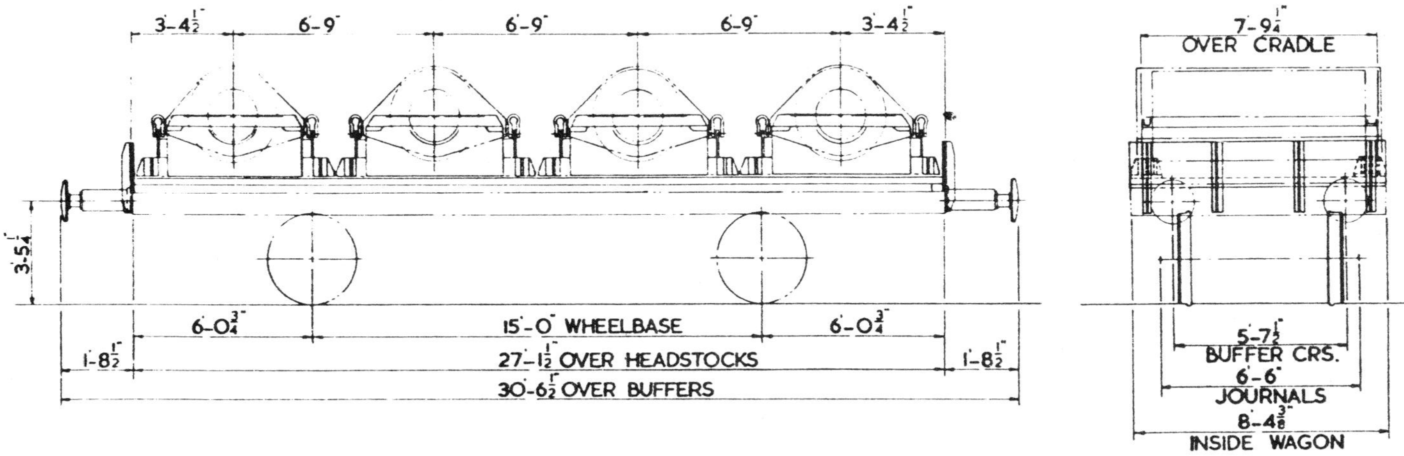


TEL CODE:- COIL F
※ TARE:- 12TONS 9CWT.
MIN CURVE:- 1½ CHAINS
BRAKE:- AVB & HAND LEVER

CRADLES:- STEEL
FLOOR:- WOOD
BUFFERS:- HYDRAULIC
BUFFER HEADS:- 1'-4" DIA.

WHEELS:- 3'-1½"
JOURNALS:- 4⅞" DIA.
AXLEBOXES:- ROLLER BEARING
COUPLINGS:- INSTANTER

※ TARE INCLUDES WEIGHT OF FOUR CRADLES.

12

Above: A Coil R No B936069 for coiled steel rod. New sides and ends have been fitted to the BR clasp vacuum brake underframe which has roller bearings, plate axleguards and Oleo-pneumatic buffers. The underframe is black and the body, including the cradles and floor battens, is bauxite. *P. W. Bartlett*

Above right: Coil E No B935227 with extended T-section stanchions welded to the originals. The BR clasp vacuum brake underframe has Hybox roller bearings, plate axleguards and Oleo-pneumatic buffers. *P. W. Bartlett*

Right: Experimental pallet wagon for animal feed No B932555 at Avonmouth Dock in 1966. The body is plywood with steel ends. The BR clasp vacuum brake underframe has roller bearings, plate axleguards and Dowty hydraulic buffers. *P. W. Bartlett Collection*

## Coil R

The 'Coil Rs' ('KRV' on TOPS) are a conversion which carries coiled steel rod from the steelworks at Cardiff and Scunthorpe. Photograph 12 shows one of these and only the vacuum braked 'Plate' underframe and floor remains. The steel ends are rcplaccd by two horizontal planks and four stanchions which extend upwards. The sides are replaced by five vertical stanchions which support a full length strip of steel channel which is at an angle. The floor has four lengthwise battens in which the coils rest. The underframe is black and the bodywork bauxite but, sometimes, the end planks are unpainted. Examples are B934915, B934921, B935070, B935938, B936159 and B936241. These wagons continue in use.

## Coil E-KEV

The 'Coil E' ('KEV' on TOPS) is similar to the 'Coil R' and also carries coiled steel rod. They were introduced more recently and are a simpler conversion in that they retain all of their 'Plate' features and simply have the four stanchions at each end extended upwards. The two central stanchions are connected across the top. Photograph 13 illustrates these features. The wagons are conventionally painted with bauxite bodies and some, for example B935602, have bauxite solebars and headstocks. At least 194 of these wagons have been converted and they work with the 'Coil Rs' from Cardiff GKN works. Conversions are from diagrams 1/431, 1/432 and 1/434 and other examples are B931134, B931301, B931602, B932223, B932890, B933019, B933489, B935525 and B936500.

## Experimental Pallet Wagon

In 1966, B932555, was converted experimentally to carry palletised bags of animal feed from the BOCM mill at Avonmouth Docks. Photograph 14 shows the distinctive features of this design. There are nine high side panels which lift away for loading. Three triangular steel rod supports hold these panels in place. There is also an inter-

13

14

nal steel frame with two vertical supports and a full length rod across the top at the sides as well as a fixed tarpaulin bar along the mid-line. The ends are high and fixed. One end has wire steps up to the tarpaulin bar, two vertical and two cross bracing strips and an internal false end which is pushed in by four screws to hold the pallets firmly in place. This arrangement is similar to that used on the more familiar 'Palbrick' wagons. The other end is of plain plywood with two T-shaped upright stanchions. The wagon carried five pairs of pallets. No similar wagons were developed from this prototype and the fate of the wagon is not known.

15

**Above: A Plaice ballast wagon No DB 987193 built at Horwich in 1979. The LNER vacuum braked underframe has roller bearings, plate axleguards and side-web buffers. The underframe is black and the body olive green with yellow step bar.** *P. W. Bartlett*

**Plaice**

The final conversion which we wish to discuss is the most recent and is likely to be the longest-lived. At present BR engineers use a vast fleet of ex open merchandise wagons to carry spoil, used ballast, short pieces of rail etc. In 1977 Horwich works built four experimental 'PLAICE' wagons ('ZCV' on TOPS) numbered DB987100-987103 to lot 3929. These were followed by an essentially similar production batch of 200 wagons to lot 3970 which were built at Horwich during 1979 and numbered DB987104-987303. Photograph 15 is of one of these wagons. As can be seen the vacuum-braked 'Plate' underframe has an entirely new body built upon it. This has a fixed end which has four rectangular section upright stanchions, a lamp iron and, on the production batch, a grab handle and two electrification warning signs. The sides drop as four doors with removable upright stanchions between each. The solid part of this side is lower than the total height of the end, but the supporting stanchions are all continued upwards to a horizontal bar. This is at the same height as the end. When the sides are dropped down this bar is used as a step-bar to give puchase when shovelling spoil into the wagon.

Examples with the LNER clasp-brake underframe are DB987100, DB987103, DB987116 and DB987193, examples with the BR clasp-brake underframe are DB987117 and DB987135. The wagons have black underframes and olive green bodies with white lettering. On the production batch the lettering is in the now conventional white boxes and the step-bar is yellow (which may make it difficult to see in the photo).

**Modelling**

At present the modelling of any of these wagons in 4mm scale would required scratchbuilding. Some suitable parts are available from well known sources such as ABS and Kenline. Oleo-pneumatic buffers are available from the Southern Railway Group and plate back axleguards from both the Scalefour and EM gauge societies.

Finally, we hope that you have found some of the foregoing of interest. As we have intimated we do not have full details of some of the conversions discussed and also expect that we have omitted some. We would be pleased to hear from anyone who has further details of these. The longevity of this design and their versatility for adaption makes them particularly interesting. However, they are not unique in this, as BR adapts many of its wagons, so keep an eye open on the passing freight scene and try and identify other conversions. We would like to thank Don Farmborough of BRHSG for supplying some of the data used in this article and Roger Silsbury for printing some of the photographs.

# BR Mk I Full Brake

**Top: No M80725 as built in red and cream livery.**

**Above: No M81125 in blue and grey livery and branded for 'BRUTE' circuit working.** *C. J. Tuffs*

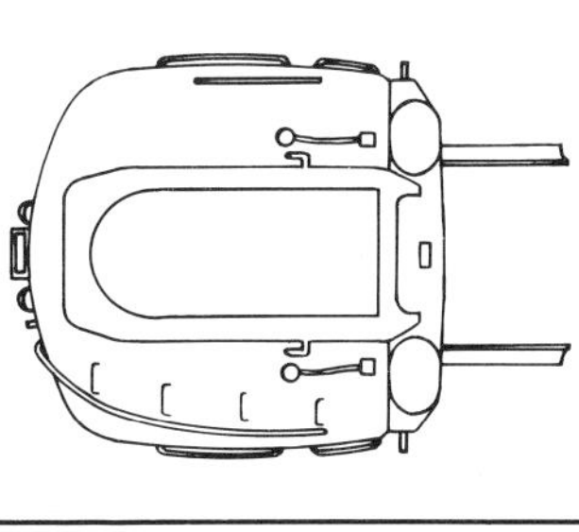

*Drawing 3   mm:1ft scale*

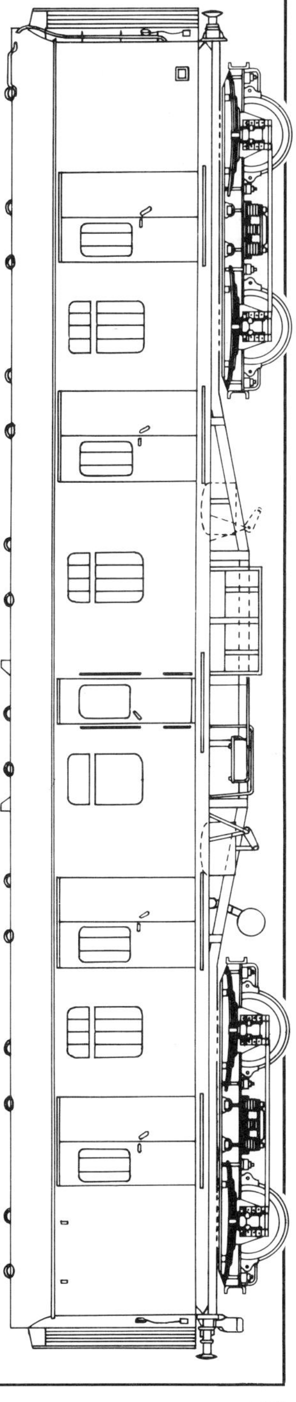

# Light activated level crossing warning lights

*A. Pugh*

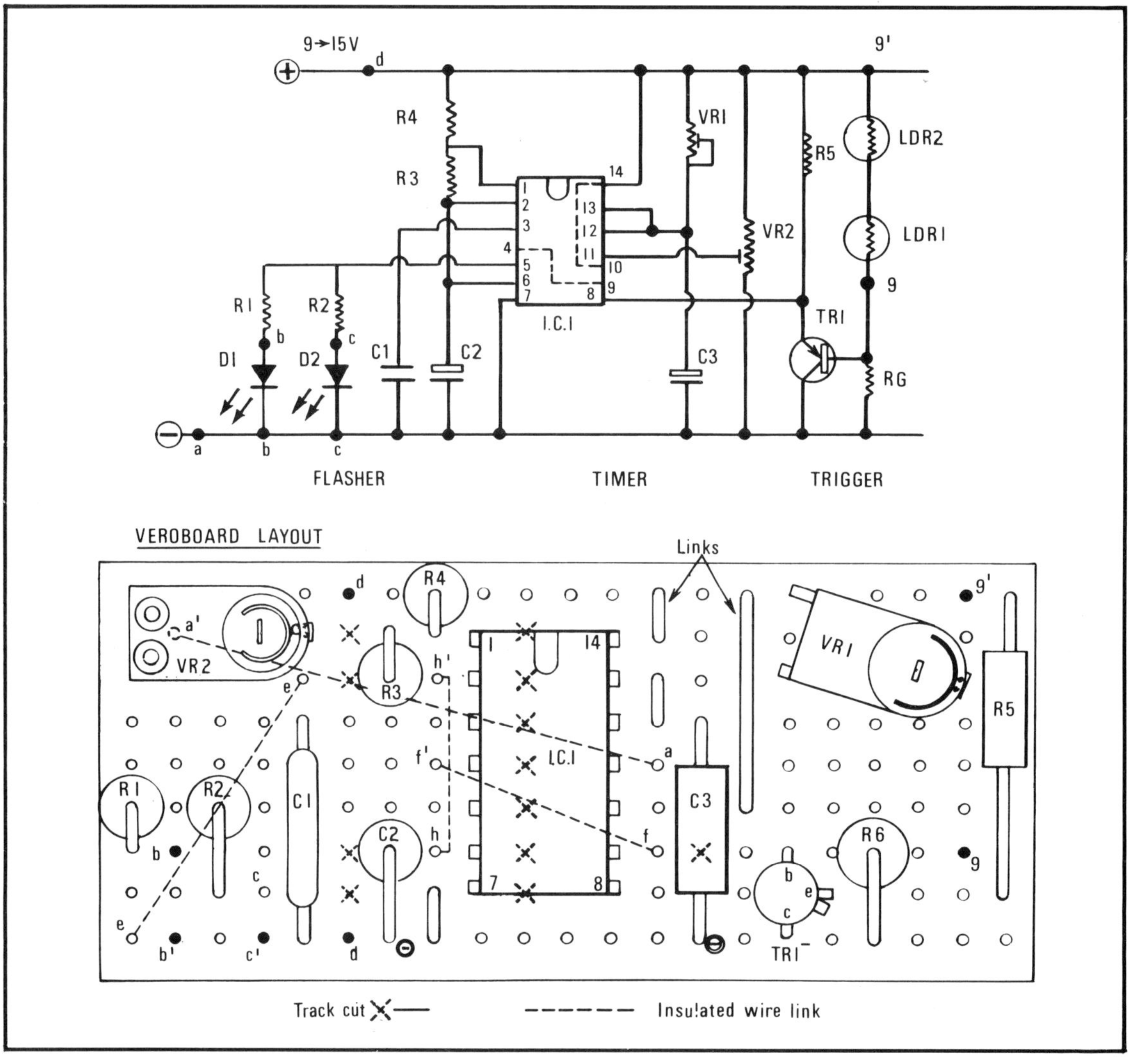

This circuit was initially conceived to automatically switch on a pair of flashing lights on a level crossing, then, after a predetermined time, switch them off again.

**How it works**

TR1, R5, R6 and the Light Dependent Resistors (LDR) form a 'dark' activated switch. Under light conditions the LDRs have low resistance (500 ohms) and the voltage developed across them is small. Since this forms the base bias for TR1 the transistor is held off (non-conducting). TR1 emitter voltage is high and therefore the voltage on pin 8.

When the train passes over either LDR its resistance increases, biasing on TR1 and causing the voltage on pin 8 of the ic to fall.

The right hand side of the ic is connected as a monostable. The fall in voltage on pin 8 flips the output on pin 9 from zero to about +5V, where it stays for a time determined by the time constant C3VR1.

The left hand side of the chip is connected as an astable which is enabled when pin 4 goes high. Its output is taken via R1 and R2 to the light emitting diodes D1 and D2. The frequency of the flashing is determined by the values of C2 and R4. With the values shown it is approximately 1Hz.

The LDRs should be mounted under the track in a hole cut between the sleepers. The sensitivity of the circuit is adjusted by VR2 so that only complete coverage of the sensor by the train triggers the lights whilst any stray shadows are ignored.

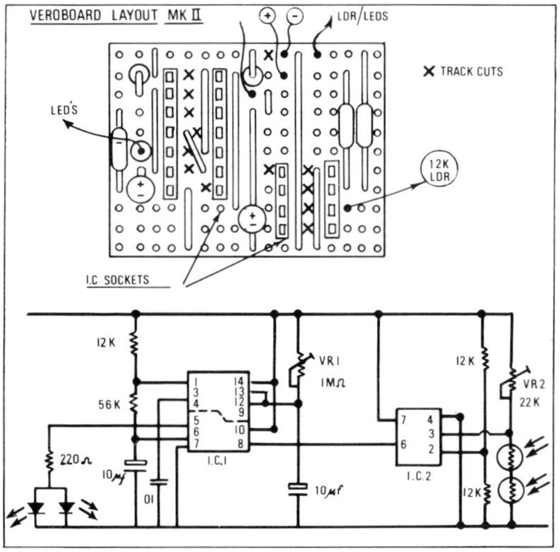


The whole circuit can be fitted on to a piece of 0.1in veroboard 9 tracks wide and 21 holes long. Points a, $a^1$; e, $e^1$ and f, $f^1$ should be connected by insulated wire (see diagram).

Point d is the +ve input.
Point $d^1$ is the – input.
Point g, $g^1$ are the take off leads to the LDRs.
Point b, $b^1$ are the take off leads to the LEDs.

The easiest mistake to make with veroboard is to forget to make the cuts in the track, in this case there are only five other than those between the ic pins.

Capacitors C2 and C3 are polarised and care should be taken to connect them the correct way.

| *Components* | *Value* | *Colour code* |
|---|---|---|
| R1, R2 | 470 | yellow violet brown |
| R3 | 68K | blue grey orange |
| R4 | 12K | brown red orange |
| R5 | 27K | red violet orange |
| R6 | 2K2 | red red red |

*All resistors ¼ Watt*

| | | |
|---|---|---|
| C1 | 0.01uf | |
| C2, C3 | 10uf | LDRs are ORP 12 |
| IC1 | 556 Timer | LEDS use minis for N-gauge |
| TR1 | BC 478 | LEDs use 0.2in for OO-gauge |
| VR1 | 1M | |
| VR2 | 10K | |

The estimated total cost is about £4.10. The greatest part of this is the LDRs at £1.00 each. If they were replaced by sets of normally closed contacts mechanically opened by the train the project could be even cheaper.

In the prototype the LEDs were incorporated in a length of thin copper tubing and fashioned to look like lamp posts.

The LDRs are placed either side of the crossing so as to trigger the lights from either direction. The distance will depend on the individual layout, as will the timer setting.

**Mark II**

Arnold, my exhibitionist colleague (whichever way you interpret that you'd be correct) ran some field tests on the Mark I and found it reliable on all but one of the sites. This particular one had extremely poor lighting.

I pointed out that a dark activated switch can only work if it is first and continuously bathed in light. Ever the perfectionist, a trait that seems common among modellers, he insisted I try to improve the circuit, hence the Mark II.

The timer circuitry remains the same, I have simply replaced the transistor circuit with an Op-Amp circuit. The output of the Op-Amp remains high as long as pin 3 input is at a lower potential than pin 2 input. VR2 is adjusted until the flasher operates then turned back $\frac{1}{4}$ turn, ensuring that the switch is on the threshold of activation. When either of the LDRs is shaded the voltage on pin 3 rises above pin 2 and the output (pin 6) falls to zero, causing the timer circuit to operate and the LEDs to flash.

One practical point to bear in mind when soldering the LEDs is that they are particularly susceptible to damage from overheating, so always use a heat shunt.

This particular veroboard layout was an attempt at miniaturisation and will fit in one of the standard plastic boxes along with a PP3 battery.

| *Approximate total cost:* | £ p |
|---|---|
| IC1 556 | 0.76 |
| IC2 741 | 0.35 |
| LDRs ORP12 | 1.96 |
| Pots | 1.00 |
| Caps | 0.20 |
| Res | 0.17 |
| LEDs | 0.50 |
| Box | 0.84 |
| | £5.78 |

**Below left: A typical modern level crossing warning light arrangement.** *N. A. Hunt*

**Below: The Mk2 system installed on an exhibition layout but virtually invisible.**

# An introduction to departmental coaches

*John Rimmer*

It is altogether a happy circumstance that a journey by rail in the 1980s may still bring the sight of passenger coaches designed for the big four pre-Nationalisation companies, and in a range of colours so catholic as to suggest the nursery train set. At the present time the British Rail coaching stock livery is more unified than ever before, and yet the vehicles in question can be black, brown, olive, grey, green, maroon, signal red, yellow, blue and red, and blue and yellow; some, timidly enough, wear the standard blue or blue and grey.

It is a fact that British Rail's fleet of departmental coaches is alive and well, though the number and the marvellous variety of its members grows less year by year. However, more than three decades after nationalisation several hundred railway coaches of earlier origin are still

**Below: The LMS vehicles dating from the 1920s which formed the wiring train for part of the Euston-Glasgow electrification programme and to which the author refers. Nearest the camera is No DM395693.** *British Railways*

playing a useful role and in addition to these are many more vehicles of BR design.

It is my intention in this essay to attempt to list some of their typical functions, and to suggest 'rules' of departmental numbering and colour, and vehicle type; although as far as these rules are concerned we shall see that departures from a simple structure are not uncommon. I would suggest that in the departmental vehicle we can find one of the most valuable examples of living railway history.

Of course departmental coaches are hardly unknown. Preservation groups have often found the departmental fleet a rich source of older vehicles (though few have escaped modification in departmental service) when sister coaches have long since disappeared from revenue earning stock. The average enthusiast, too, can hardly fail to be aware of them, particularly as today he is more tuned to the railway scene as a whole than was his counterpart of a couple of decades or more ago; many now collect coach numbers, and tend to record a train rather than merely an engine.

What, precisely, is a departmental coach?

For the purposes of this discussion it is a passenger stock vehicle (although not necessarily passenger carrying), which has been withdrawn from revenue earning stock and taken up new duties with one of the railway's ancillary departments, such as those of the Chief Civil Engineer (CCE) or the Chief Mechanical and Electrical Engineer (CM&EE). In a few cases only, vehicles have entered departmental stock and have later returned to the main fleet. Some sleepers of LMS design carry prominent lettering 'On loan to CCE LMR'.

If there is one new role which is more common than any other it is the conversion of a coach to a messing/living/tool van which will accompany a piece of machinery such as a breakdown crane or track machine. Otherwise departmental duties are legion and also included in the fleet are such vehicles as cell trucks (for transporting batteries), stores and 'Enparts' vans which carry materials between works and depots, observation saloons and track recording coaches, mobile classrooms, heater vans, weighing machine maintenance vans, overhead (electric wire) maintenance trains, mobile laboratories, and cinema coaches. This list is far from definitive but will perhaps serve to indicate the variety of types.

In the case of crane runners, and also the reel flats which accompany overhead maintenance trains, the initial conversion has been so extreme

**Below: An ex-GWR Hawksworth coach in use as a staff vehicle with a Neptune track recorder.** *C. J. Marsden*

**Right: Another Hawksworth vehicle, accompanying a ballast cleaner.** *C. J. Marsden*

**Below right: Ex-LSWR brake third as mobile first aid unit at Feltham in 1960s.** *Chris Leigh*

as to remove all the original bodywork. In the majority of other conversions the interior of the vehicle has been stripped completely. Mess vans will commonly have been refitted with an iron stove and longitudinal benches and tables; in austere succession to the soft furnishings which once played their part in wooing the fare paying passenger.

In the light of the necessary conversions it is not surprising that a popular choice of vehicle for departmental service is the brake-ended corridor coach (though with gangways customarily removed) in which part of the vehicle is already open and thus requires less alteration. Corridor coaches do not possess the full width transverse partitions of suburban stock, which would surely be a nuisance in most departmental roles. Nevertheless there are numbers of non-corridor coaches to be found in the departmental fleet, though they form a relatively small percentage of the total fleet.

As a further general reflection on vehicle types, it may be considered odd that few full brakes have ever found their way into service use, though they would seem to be very well suited for the majority of duties. It is true that the BR Mk 1 full brakes have been subject to very few withdrawals from capital stock as yet. On the other hand, many full brakes of pre-1948 design have gone for scrap in good condition and apparently requiring little work to equip them as departmental tool vans.

In connection with the principal duties listed earlier, it is noteworthy that certain non-passenger coaching stock types have become identified with particular departmental roles. Thus, some 40 LMS 6-wheel fish vans still survive as departmental stores vans. Unusually

**Above: Also at Feltham was this early LSWR full brake, as a stores van.** *Chris Leigh*

**Left: An ex-GWR four-wheeler in Departmental service at Aberystwyth about 1966.** *Chris Leigh*

for departmental coaching stock these vehicles retain their original numbers in the M40xxx series, although with the addition of departmental prefix letters, of which more later. Similarly, many GWR siphon Gs have been translated into enparts vehicles numbered in the DB975xxx range, and Pooley weighing machine maintenance vans, at least on the Midland Region, have long been the preserve of ex-LNWR 6-wheel CCTs. These last, having survived upward of six decades, must be numbered among the oldest vehicles on British Rail, though they are currently being replaced by standard goods vans.

Otherwise the origin of types in the departmental fleet is very wide, and of considerable interest in indicating just which kinds of coach were being withdrawn from revenue-earning stock at the time. The majority of the LMR fleet of overhead maintenance train flat-roofed conversions were LMS '2 window' style coaches of 1920s construction, which were being taken out of use around 1960. These electrification coaches occupy most of the DM 3956xx, range, while higher numbers in the DM 395xxx fleet tend to be the province of Stanier designed coaches from the mid-1930s on, taken into the departmental fleet around the early to mid-1960s. They, in their turn, were disappearing from passenger use under the triple pressure of old age, a dwindling passenger network, and a huge fleet of BR Mk 1 coaches, the older members of which were themselves succumbing in the same decade.

It should here be mentioned that departmental coaches currently in existence, whether of BR or earlier origin, for the most part only entered departmental service in BR days. This is not to say that the old companies did not possess departmental vehicles, but such vehicles have, unhappily, long since gone. Some of them were of great interest and antiquity.

The various colours of departmental coaching stock have been referred to, and it is worth pointing out that these colours often have their own significance. Thus breakdown train (BTU) vehicles are bright red or, in cases of more recent conversion or repaint, yellow. Research vehicles are usually red and blue, with the red in place of the light grey of current BR livery. Observation saloons and track recording coaches are usually blue and grey as in normal practice, understandably in the case of the latter, as they are attached to passenger trains in normal service.

The Eastern and Western Regions tend to favour black or green for large numbers of coaches in their fleets, whilst these colours are rarely to be found on the Southern or London Midland Regions which prefer variations on a drab range which runs from olive green to purplish brown. Departmental coaches are 'shopped' at the major carriage works, but it is possible to encounter strange and presumably unofficial repaints. For example, DM 395895, a CCE vehicle based at Watford has recently been painted in mid-grey colour, but with the window framing left in its previous brown livery. A rather more extreme case is provided by DM 395831, which accompanies a District Engineers crane. When seen at Walsall in August 1979 it was sporting black lower bodysides and brown upper body broken by yellow window framing and droplights. One half of the roof was daubed with a blotchy coat of white, as though the painter's good intentions had evaporated in the face of the remaining acreage. The coach looked something less than dignified in its shoddy harlequin garb, and indeed it may be argued that a sober workmanlike livery is best suited to such vehicles. Two instruction cars, Nos DM 395227/8, which were withdrawn from Derby in 1979 and scrapped by Chadwicks of Warrington, were graced by the former BR livery of maroon lined in black and gold, and they provided a poignant reminder of past glories.

One frustration, and perhaps perversely an attraction, of the departmental fleet is that there are no published lists of types, numbers and locations in anything like a complete state. The Railway Correspondence and Travel Society does print monthly notes on departmental coaching stock in the *Railway Observer* but for the most part, new sightings are unexpected and probably rather more appealing for that.

It may be useful at this point to summarise the major numbering blocks used for departmental coaches:-

It is usual for the vehicle to carry a number containing up to six digits, most commonly six, which is preceded by letters. Where there are only two prefix letters the first is D (for departmental); the second is then an indication of the owning region, thus we then have DE, DM, DS and DW. This second, regional letter also usually conforms to the vehicle's design origin — for example practically all DM vehicles are of LMS or LMS constituent design. An additional second letter in use since 1966 when it replaced the earlier regional prefixes is 'B' which denotes standard BR vehicles.

However, to increase the complexity of the code somewhat, a third letter, more widely employed in recent years, may precede the two

**Below: The ultimate Departmental vehicle, No DB999550, the high-speed track recording car converted from a Mk 2 coach.** *BR*

letters already mentioned. This letter indicates the vehicle's purpose, or more properly its owning department, as follows:

- A Chief Mechanical and Electrical Engineer
- C British Rail Engineering Ltd
- K Chief Signal and Telecommunications Engineer
- L CM&EE Electrical Construction
- O Observation Saloon
- R Research Department
- T Operating Division
- Z BR Publicity

Other letters, P (for Shipping and Internal Services) and X (for Stores) are rarely, if ever, used for departmental coaches. The absence of any of the above letters should indicate that the vehicle is part of the Chief Civil Engineer's stock, although in practice many coaches should bear one of the above letters, but do not. The following are the main blocks of numbers:

DM 3950xx through to the early 3960xxs
DE 320xxx to at least 3211xx
DS 1 to DS1xxx and DS 700xx to DS 703xx
DW 9xxx and DW 150xxx to at least DW 1504xx
DB 9750xx up to DB 9759/99 and 977000 onwards

There were earlier numbering schemes, usually of pre-nationalisation origins, and amongst these were DM 19xxxx (for example DM 198755, a stores van of LNWR design), and DE 9xxxxx (Nos 910042 and 940485 were both inspection saloons). Some WR observation saloons in the W809xx series still survive, while BR-built inspection saloons are numbered in the 9995xx series.

**Above: Ex-LNER Gresley coach No ADE 320905 as a staff van at Wath in 1980.** *P. Harris*

**Above right: An elderly 6-wheeler as a cinema coach generator van at Willesden in 1960.** *A. Swain*

These last display a fascinating range of alternative prefix letters, as the following demonstrate: TODM 999501, TDB 999502, DBM 999504, DB 999508/9.

Otherwise subsidiary departmental numbering schemes are still quite varied. The fact that some vans retain their original running-stock numbers has been mentioned and Midland Region heater vans have a number series to themselves in ADM 444xx. A few BR suburban coaches carry numbers DB 963xxx and at least some of these had been brakes on Freightliner trains.

So far we have been dealing with coaches which, in theory at least, have the run of the whole BR system. It is important also to recognise the existence of the Internal User fleet, which is made up of vehicles which are confined to particular locations and are not allowed to roam freely on the main lines. In this further complication of numbering systems there are no prefix letters. The fleets are:

Midland Region Internal User 02xxxx
Eastern Region Internal User 04xxxx
Western Region Internal User 06xxxx and 07xxxx
Southern Region Internal User 08xxxx
Scottish Region Internal User 09xxxx

It should be pointed out that quite a few freight stock vehicles (usually goods vans) are included in these lists, which have not been superseded by a 'National' version like the DB code.

Although this essay is in some peril of being immersed in numbers and numbering systems it should be helpful to list some coaches which conform to the basic rules:

ADM 395205
ex-LMS coach, extensively repanelled, red livery, BTU Tool Van allocated to Crewe.

CDM 395285
ex-LMS CCT, drab livery, Cell Truck

KDM 395414
ex-LMS Brake Second No M22716. Since withdrawn, this was a Signal Engineers Staff Coach based at Blackburn. Drab livery

ADE 320391
ex-LNER Third No E82447 BTU tool van, since withdrawn. Red.

LDE 320542
flat-roofed coach with replanked body. Electrification, cantilever and assembly vehicle. Scottish Region. Black livery. Currently at work on Bedford-St Pancras electrification.

ADS 70090/1
ex-SR emu cars S8446/5. De-icing set No 012. Blue livery. Recently withdrawn and sent to Armytage of Chesterfield.

KDS 13
ex-SR PMV. Staff and tool van (Signal Engineers). Drab livery.

TDS 70159
ex SR Maunsell coach. 'Office'. Drab livery.

KDW 9922
ex-GWR coach. Signal Engineers staff coach, recently withdrawn and sent to F. Berry of Leicester from Carmarthen. Black livery.

DW 150338
ex-GWR coach which travels with a ballast cleaning machine. Blue livery.

RDB 975136
ex-BR Mk 1 corridor brake second M34505. Laboratory No 12. Red/blue livery.

ZDB 975403
ex-BR Mk 1 coach. Cinema coach. Blue/grey.

024312
ex-LMS. Full brake M31051. Internal User, Wolverton Works. Blue.

083181
ex-ADS 70201, ex-SR Open third S1346. Instruction coach at Clapham Junction. Drab livery.

Coaches which bend the rules a little include KDB 975094, which was actually LMS corridor brake third M26610M; but there are other examples of vehicles of company origin which were transferred to departmental stock after the introduction of the DB series. ADM 320158 ex-corridor brake third E43272, a BTU tool van (since scrapped) had somehow acquired an 'M' prefix in front of its correct Eastern Region number. Similarly Lincoln's BTU tool and packing van is currently numbered TDB 320612. Others are DM 395699K and DWM 150297. One wonders how many such apparent aberrations result from an 'unofficial' hand at work as in the case of the irregular repaints.

Mention of the Crewe and Lincoln BTU vehicles may serve to introduce the matter of allocations, and in the case of BTU coaches they are allocated to a particular depot, although subject to occasional reallocations as with locomotives.

**Above: A specially constructed departmental saloon No W 80943W at Old Oak Common in 1967.**
*K. P. Lawrence*

Such vehicles become familiar landmarks and it is with regret that one notes their withdrawal.

Other vehicles, particularly those which accompany various machines apart from breakdown units, are more extensively travelled and one might encounter the same specimen at several widely spaced points over a relatively short period of time. However, alongside BTU coaches, there are those others which become rooted in a particular location, and one might cite here the two ex-GWR coaches occupied a siding to the north of Royal Oak station barely half a mile from Paddington. They were KD 9899 and DK 150205, (note the prefix!), transferred to Internal User stock as 060902/3. DM 396009 was berthed outside St Pancras station for a long time in the late 1970s, though by early 1980 it was in sorry condition at the west side of Cricklewood Yard. DM 395999 is ex-LMS GUV No M37754 outside Euston carriage shed, whilst DB 975330, ex-Mk 1 brake second corridor M34070, still wearing lined maroon was a classroom, visible at the end of Derby station. This last coach might more properly be included in the Internal User fleet as it was isolated on two tiny sections of track, one to each bogie.

As with other items of rolling stock some departmentals are deprived of their underframes and do further service as huts, like DE 320709, formerly 'Mobile Office, Doncaster DCE'. No longer mobile, it is a grounded body in the yard at Barnetby. DM 395116, and ex-LNWR CCT is used by a farmer in a field south of Kettering. However after service in both the main and departmental fleets not many vehicles would be in condition for a further spell of work. Two coaches which almost demanded to be put out of their misery were DM 395797/395081, long condemned and mouldering quietly in Wolverton yard throughout the 1970s.

Naturally, coaching stock works such as Wolverton frequently see departmental coaches in for assessment. The Southern Region made good use of the now closed South Lambeth goods yard, to the rear of Battersea power station, and conveniently adjacent to Stewarts Lane depot and works. At times there were more than a dozen SR coaches present, a few of them condemned and awaiting disposal.

We have noted earlier that the transfer of a coach to the departmental fleet may involve it in massive rebuilding, or virtually no alteration at all. In either of these extremes and in the many intermediate states it may not be easy to determine the previous identity of the vehicle. This may usually be accomplished in very broad terms, as, for instance in being able to recognise an LMS coach of Stanier's time; and by reference to more specific points (an access to background information) one can often say 'Southern Railway coach, Maunsell designed BTK of 1932'.

Builders plates often survive on the solebar and can sometimes give information of lot number and building date as well as the place of construction. The Southern Region tends to be more zealous in the application of 'rebuild' plates which replace the originals. For instance DB 975534, a viaduct inspection unit, mess and workshop was a BR Mk 1 BSK of early fifties build, No S34255. It now bares the solebar plate 'DB 975534 3 TON STEWARTS LANE 1970 LOT NO 3719'.

On happy occasions which are all too rare, and usually when the vehicle has not been repainted too often since its transfer to the departmental fleet, it is possible to decipher its original number still standing proud under the paint. DB 975534 was such a vehicle, but one normally searches in vain, and often with the realisation that the area of the bodyside in question has been repanelled. The Eastern Region, with a high incidence of wooden bodied vehicles, frequently allows departmental paintwork to deteriorate to the extent that original numbers are once again plainly visible.

That departmental coaches in their various roles will continue to be necessary seems certain. There appears to be no move toward a policy of purpose-built vehicles and it is likely that many more coaches still in the revenue earning fleet will end their days as departmentals. Meanwhile the steady withdrawal of the surviving company-designed vehicles continues, but there are still many about with over half a century's service behind them. We should feel some regret at the passing of these veterans, and at the loss of the variety which is still available to us. We might also recognise that in years to come the sight of surviving BR Mk 1 vehicles in the departmental fleet will be eagerly sought after, upon the expiry of that type in regular passenger use.

My thanks are due to Stephen Jones for his helpful comments, and to the columns of the *Railway Observer,* journal of the RCTS.

**Below: A Bulleid coach branded Es formed in a freight at Norwood Junction in 1981.** *A. Dasi-Sutton*

# Small Structures 5

# Steel girder under line culvert

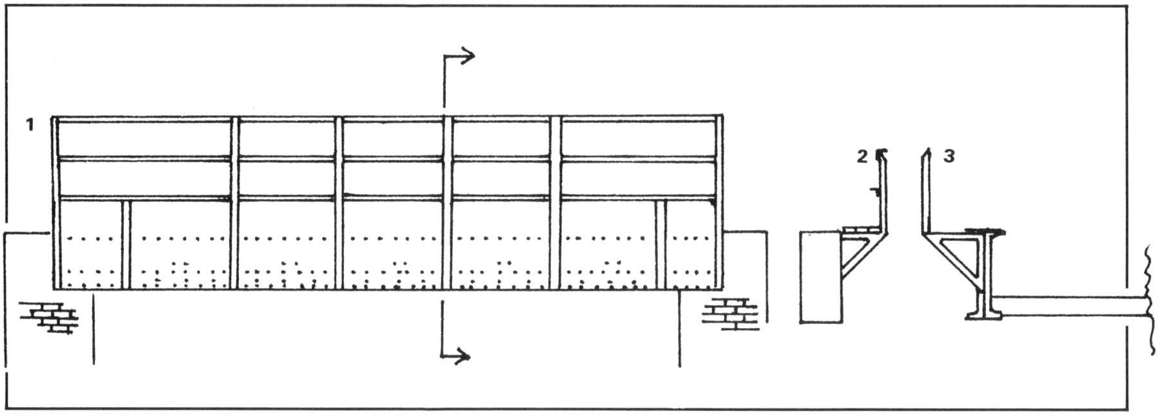


This neat little culvert bridge is typical of thousands which existed on single track railway lines throughout the UK. They were used to bridge streams, drainage channels and occupation crossings and form an ideal subject for modelling, using readily available brass sections or Plastruct and styrene sheet. The main members are two broad 'I' section girders mounted on brick piers. Small 'I' section girders are laid across the span, resting on the bottom web of the main girders and riveted in place. A steel deck plate is carried on top of these, and the track is laid and ballasted in the usual way. The railings and their stanchions are assembled from 'L' section material, the stanchions and their triangular braces being riveted to the main structure, while the railings are welded in place. A timber walkway is provided on both sides. The drawings are to 4mm:1ft scale and show one elevation and one end elevation. Fig 3 is a section through the structure as indicated by the arrows in Fig 1.

This little bridge survived into the 1980s and the line was still in regular use by Class 47s and 100 ton bogie tank wagons.

**Below and below right: Two views of this typical under-line single-track culvert.**

# Really simple track circuits

*C. P. Boocock*

Many of us like to have a tunnel or hidden sections of track on our model railways. In this way a continuous run can be disguised, or trains can be held out of sight on unseen storage sidings.

One problem with this is that the busy operator can forget where a train is standing. The resultant collision occurs in a confined space where rerailing operations are uncomfortably difficult. The operator therefore needs a reminder that a train is occupying a section.

On our model railway, Weybourne Mark II, there are two different types of hidden track where trains can be stopped. There are two dead-end sidings and a double track reverse loop, all in tunnel. With advice from two friends, Ron Puntis and Mike Yeomans, I have fitted track circuits which light up when trains are in these hidden parts.

These circuits are really very simple indeed, far more so than most electronic circuits appearing in the pages of modelling publications. They can be fitted by anybody who can solder, have only four small components each, and cost only pennies. With a track circuit in operation, a train standing in or running through a hidden section is indicated by a little red, green, or yellow light on the control panel.

What a track circuit does is to connect a very low voltage electric supply to both running rails of the track section in question, positive to one rail, negative to the other.

When a locomotive or power bogie enters the section, the low voltage current can flow from one running rail through the wheels, through the motor armature and out into the other rail thus completing the circuit and illuminating the light on the control panel. Because the track circuit is fed from a source completely separate from the traction current neither circuit seriously affects the other. The track circuit current is far too small to overheat the motor of a model, even if it is stopped in the section for hours, and the movement of trains only causes the track circuit lights to flicker slightly. Those on our layout have been in regular use for over a year and are quite successful.

Our railway uses standard 12V dc power supply for traction and the H&M controllers have extra 16V ac sockets at the side, fed from a separate winding on the transformer. From one 16V socket a wire is led via a tiny $\frac{1}{4}$ watt resistor of around 500 ohms resistance to the input leg (the longer one) of the small 2mm diameter light emitting diode (LED), fitted in a small hole in the appropriate part of the control panel track diagram. A diode is a device which permits current to flow through itself in only one direction, so it is important to wire it the right way round, otherwise the LED will not light up! The next wire is soldered to the output terminal of the LED and goes to one running rail.

From the opposite running rail a wire is run to the positive terminal of a small 20V diode. A diode of this type is small, black and cylindrical and has a white ring at the output end. The wire is soldered from the rail on to the plain end of the diode and another wire is run from the output end to the other 16V terminal on the transformer.

The purpose of the resistor is to drop the 16V ac to about 2V to suit the LED and to avoid influencing the traction current. The second diode is important in that it prevents stray circulating currents from other circuits that may be connected to the same pair of 16V terminals.

FIG.1 DEAD END SIDING TRACK CIRCUIT

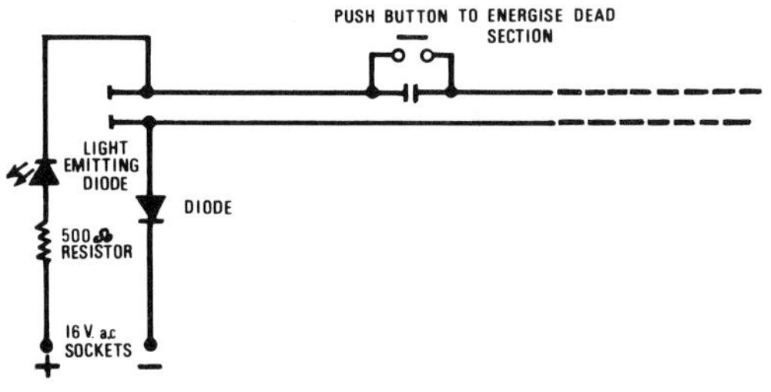


FIG.2 DOUBLE REVERSE LOOP Showing track circuit applied to outer loop

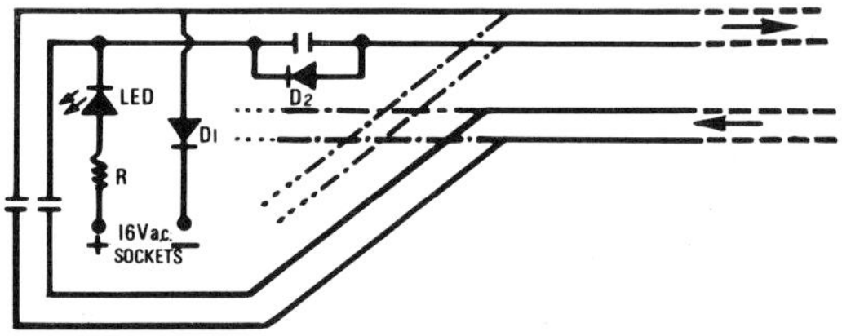


One more thing needs to be done. As the circuit has been described so far, the LED will light up whenever and wherever a train is on the track fed from that controller. It is necessary to provide means for containing the track circuit's influence to the section of track specified, so that the LED goes out when the train leaves that section.

To do this one has to cut a break into one of the running rails so that the track circuit current cannot flow once the train is past the break.

On dead-end sidings the break is easy to arrange as shown in Fig 1. Because one wants to stop the train automatically before it hits the buffer stops, one can put a rail break at the point beyond which one wants the locomotive to stop. The break can be bridged by a small push button to enable the train to be released subsequently. The track circuit remains dead until a train runs into the section and the LED lights up.

The double track reverse loop at one end of the Weybourne layout posed a problem, but this was solved as shown in Fig 2. Two controllers are used on the main line circuit and one break between them is in the reverse loop tunnel. That fixed the point of entry into the track circuit. A rail break was made in the positive rail (right hand rail in the direction of running) where the exit end of the track circuit was required. A 20V diode (D2) was soldered across the break as shown in the diagram. Now as a train enters the section the LED lights up, and it goes out as the train comes out of the tunnel. There is one slight snag. It means that trains can only run forwards through the section. Diode D2 prevents a reverse movement. If necessary this could be overcome by bridging the diode D2 with a small push button, though I've not found that to be necessary. Wrong line working is not permitted into the Weybourne tunnels!

That really is all there is to it. It has been much more difficult to describe than to instal! I can imagine that many storage loops could use this type of track circuit with advantage, as could sections at the back of engine shed, in fact almost anywhere where the operator cannot see.

Experience over the past year has been largely successful. The only snag has been that two of the resistors did overheat, due, I think, to some stray traction current. I replaced them with $\frac{1}{2}$ Watt ones (still costing only pennies) with no resultant problems.

One has to be careful with multiple unit or push-pull trains where the locomotive or power car may be at the rear. I have found that the headlights on the dummy power car of my son's HST will light this track circuit, which is helpful. Other 'driving trailer' coaches without lights will need a resistor strapped across pickups on the wheels on both sides of the leading bogie. A resistor of around 500 ohms, $\frac{1}{4}$ Watt will suffice.

The components and light wire for these circuits can be purchased from any good electronic components shop and they are very cheap. On a big layout it could be that the wire is the most expensive part of a track circuit!